EXCHANGE

Trading Your Brokenness for Exceptional Purpose

BY REV. DR. CHARLEY HAMES, JR.

SPIRITDRIVEN PUBLISHING

Spirit Driven Publishing ™

JP Designs Art, cover design

Paraclete Press, interior design

Margot Starbuck, editor

First Edition

Printed in the United States of America

This title is also available in eBook.

Library of Congress Control Number: 2017904167

ISBN: 978-1-5323-3699-7

I dedicate EXCHANGE

*to my loving grandmother, Henrietta Whirl,
who always encouraged me to keep my hand in God's hand.
Thank you for giving me an example of studying
and reading the Word of God.*

*To the five congregations that allowed me to serve you
and develop with you, it has been truly a privilege
to serve as your leader.*

*I dedicate this book also to Dr. Jerome E. McNeil,
my friend and big brother.
I dedicate this book also to Rev. Jerome B. Price Sr.,
who served as my pastor and became family.
Finally, I dedicate this book to Bishop Dotcy I. Isom Jr.,
who gave me a chance and opportunity to share
in the ministry of God's people.
These fallen soldiers have had a significant impact on my life.
I am grateful for their walk and example of faithfulness.
To God be the Glory!*

※

Contents

Preface

Exchange: Trading Your Brokenness for Exceptional Purpose was birthed from a passion to encourage people to move beyond the brokenness of their lives. So many individuals go through life hurt, mistreated, shattered, bruised, and broken, with no tools to repair the ruptures they've endured. I know this because I was one of those people who simply accepted my brokenness as part of my journey. But, graciously, God showed me that the hurts I'd suffered might describe a part of my journey, but they definitely were not the destiny God intended for me.

My purpose in writing *Exchange* was to help the reader to cultivate the desire to live beyond his or her shattered pieces by trading them for an extraordinary life. I wanted to reach the brother or sister who was standing on the edge of life, ready to leap into hopelessness because he or she wasn't convinced that his or her life mattered.

If that's you, know that God has a purpose for your life.

Writing *Exchange* stretched me mentally and spiritually because I needed to carve out time and space at a time in my life when my schedule was beyond busy. Things were going great when I felt the calling to write this book. I didn't want to revisit the emotions and memories of times when I was broken. Who does? However, each time I lay awake in bed sleepless at night, I was reminded by God of this calling and would jot notes on a writing pad or on my smartphone that sat on the side of the bed. God reminded me that He didn't allow me to endure those broken moments to keep them to myself. My brokenness became the gift I could give to encourage someone else that they, too, could trade their own brokenness for exceptional purpose.

This journey climaxed in 2016 when I felt a burden to finish this project like never before. This book helped me to be mindful of the purpose for which God called me: to serve others. This book is my feeble attempt to remain faithful to the calling that God placed on my life. Writing this book changed me for the better, and now I hope it will do the same for you!

I want to thank and acknowledge several individuals who helped me make this project possible. I want to thank Dr. John Ortberg, whom I called in a pinch with editing needs, who had his daughter on speed dial to rescue me from my editing stress. I would also like to thank his gracious daughter, Laura Turner, who was available to help, as her father had assured me. She guided me to Margot Starbuck, a fantastic editor who demonstrated patience, resilience, and diligence in making my project her priority. She's the G.O.A.T—greatest of all time! Her skillset and expertise is five-star, and her execution is phenomenal.

I would like to thank Sarah Kovac who proofread this work, making it ready for publication. I want to thank John Paul Moore for his genius creativity and unique ability make our vision a reality for my book cover. I want to thank my son, Charles Jonathon, who became my sounding board, helping me with the last rounds of title changes. And I want to thank all my children for being patient with me through the hours of writing that their sacrifices made possible. I want to thank my amazingly brilliant and strikingly beautiful wife, who was understanding and gracious through this process. Finally, I want to thank all of the churches that I've served as pastor and also the Christian Methodist Episcopal Church for providing the opportunity to be used by the Master.

I have prayed that you find something in each chapter that will bless your life.

Now let's get ready to exchange.

CHAPTER 1

Cracks and Chips

"Go ahead and label me, because labels are made for gifts."

–Robert M. Hensel

I remember that fateful recess like it was yesterday.

It was a fresh, sunny day. The grass was green, the sky was blue, the sun was shining, and I couldn't wait to go outside for recess. I thought we were going to play dodge ball, but there was no ball available. So we were left to our own devices. The teachers were on the playground, but they were deeply engrossed in their conversations. One of my classmates suggested, "Hey guys, let's play 'The Dozens.'"

The Dozens was a game of words spoken between two people who insulted each other until the other person gave up. This game was played in front of the players' friends while they laughed at their buddy's expense.

The Dozens never ended well.

The first two players, whom I'll call Tray and Chris, unleashed insults like a water hose on a blazing fire. Everybody seemed to be enjoying the creative insults until one of my classmates said two words that caused a cataclysmic shift on the playground that morning.

Tray was offended because Chris called him broke. As the word rolled off Chris's lips, Tray's face turned dark and rage began to rise from his pores. When I saw the flash of anger on his face, I knew bad was about to happen.

To drive his point home, Chris added, "You are so broke that you are broken!"

And then Tray unleashed the two-word arsenal that moved heaven and earth by retorting, "Yo Momma!"

Time stood still as every eye turned to Chris to see what he would do. Well, actually, we knew exactly what he'd do. And when he took that first swing at Tray, the group of boys gathered went wild. All of us who were on the playground that morning playing the Dozens got in trouble.

"Yo Momma" simply wasn't something you said back in that day without causing rifts in relationship. These two words were a declaration of defeat for the other person because "Yo Momma" was the ultimate insult. Nothing was more offensive than for a friend or enemy to disrespect the person who birthed you and gave you life. An opponent could make cracks about the off-brand shoes you were wearing, the second-hand clothing you may have been dressed in, or even the house in which you lived. You could even talk smack about people's cousins, aunts, and uncles. You might even get away with talking about their father. But it was common knowledge that you couldn't say *anything* about somebody's mother.

I remember being curious about what made Tray, who was called "broken," respond the way he did. It certainly wasn't the ultimate insult. In fact, there were some pretty ugly things spoken that day that made "broken" sound like a bedtime story. I'm not sure what went through Tray's mind on that day, but I do know that Chris's jab set him off. And, after that, I started to notice that no one I knew wanted to be associated with being broken.

So what does it mean to be broken? Broken is an adjective that means being fractured or damaged and no longer in one piece or working order. Maybe when you hear this definition it's easy to think of a few people who qualify! You may feel confident that you know folks like this, but the description certainly doesn't fit you. That's because we typically don't see ourselves as being broken. And if someone suggests that we are, we immediately become defensive and dismissive. The first thing that many of us will announce to our accusers is, "I am not broken!"

Who wants to be broken?

Brokenness

Brokenness comes in countless shapes and sizes.

You may be feeling broken today if the love of your life betrayed your trust.

If you've lost a child or a spouse to death, you may be searching for a reason to keep living.

Maybe you were months from retirement at a job where you served faithfully for twenty-five years, but when the company was purchased, your position was "phased out."

Maybe you've graduated with a specialized degree but your student loan debt is choking the life out of you because you have been unable to find a job.

Or maybe you're feeling broken because your dreams for your life haven't been realized the way you hoped they would be.

No one wants to be associated with something that is damaged. No one intends to have a broken heart, a broken relationship, a broken marriage, a broken vow, a broken career, a broken home, or even broken bones. But the harsh reality is that many of us have. All of us can, on some level, identify with feeling broken. Perhaps you've not been smashed to pieces, but you may have incurred some cracks and chips throughout your life.

A friendship has been broken.

A parent has suffered an illness.

A marriage is strained.

A child makes unwise choices.

A spouse is gripped by addiction.

The sting of brokenness can even be felt when you're picked last for the basketball team in high school gym class!

Among the countless people I've encountered on my journey, I've met many who have chosen to live with their cracks and chips rather than seeking to be healed. And though they fail to recognize them, their cracks are apparent to others. Though life has split them, they've learned how to function by hanging on without fully separating. I called this "functioning in dysfunction."

Many are engaged in relationships that are no longer meaningful or fulfilling. Perhaps a man works for a supervisor who belittles him, and has limited his opportunity for advancement, but he doesn't have the courage or the internal resources to walk away. Someone else has been cracked by scathing critiques and feels that she is never good enough. Maybe this one has served in her church for years, helping to grow the ministry, and no one has ever offered a simple, "Thank you." Others have heard these condemning words: "Your daddy wasn't nothing and you won't amount to anything." They look for validation only to find themselves rejected over and over again by those who were responsible for nurturing their well-being. Or maybe someone had a gift that was celebrated—athletic ability, a gift for speaking, a beautiful singing voice—but they never learned to develop strength of character alongside their obvious talent. Chipped by misery and cracked by mayhem, many have resigned themselves to believing that they have no other choice than to live broken.

There are some who don't know that they are broken. And if they don't know, they don't know. However, it's important to become as self-aware as possible. Yes, brokenness is real, but it doesn't have to be one's way of life. Reality can be painful to deal with, but it's important to understand that the cracks and chips in our lives have a purpose. If we never identify the brokenness, we can never get to the place of being unbroken.

Clay Jars

So how do you begin to face the brokenness in yourself and begin to recognize that reality as a blessing? It begins with an honest assessment of yourself and your situation. When you're willing to do that hard work, things can begin to change in your life.

One adage moved me to own my truth. It says, "Life doesn't come with a remote control. You have to get up and change it yourself."

Many of us don't want to take an in-depth look at our lives for fear that it might confirm what others have said about us. Don't worry about what they are saying about you. Just begin to concentrate on becoming the best version of you!

The first step to exchanging brokenness for extraordinary purpose is surveying all of the areas in your life that are fractured. I want you to take an honest look at every chipped, cracked, and damaged place in your life that keeps you from fulfilling your potential. Let me caution you that the moment you start acknowledging the imperfections in your "jar," the enemy will try to convince you that there is something wrong with you. I want to reassure you that there is nothing wrong with you that's outside of God's power to transform. In fact, I would suggest that, as you face your brokenness, you are already moving in the direction of healing and wholeness.

Though the enemy will try to convince you that there is something inherently faulty and unredeemable within you, don't forget that the devil is a liar. Remember the words of David: "You have made them a little lower than the angels and crowned them with glory and honor" (Ps. 8:5). Because God created you in his image, you are altogether worthy. Despite your brokenness, what was true when you were formed is still true now.

The Apostle Paul, in the New Testament, describes the way God uses us with all of our chips and cracks and fissures and breaks. In his second letter to the church at Corinth, Paul exhorts,

> "But we have this treasure in jars of clay to show that this all-surpassing power is from God and not from us. We are hard pressed on every side, but

not crushed; perplexed, but not in despair; persecuted, but not abandoned; struck down, but not destroyed" (2 Cor. 4:7-9 NIV).

The jars Paul refers to were jars that were cheaply made and would be prone to cracks and chips. Earthenware vessels were commonplace in virtually every home in the ancient Middle East. They were inexpensive and easily broken. Unlike metal vessels, which could be repaired, or glass ones, which could be melted down and reused, earthenware vessels had to be discarded once they were broken. They had little intrinsic value. Everyday people would store grain, hide valuables, and keep oil for their lamps in these ordinary earthenware vessels.

Specifically, Paul may have had in mind the small, earthenware oil lamps sold so cheaply in the marketplace. If so, the apostles were the frail human vessels that held the treasure: the light of the gospel made to shine through them into the world's darkness.

We naturally expect that such a precious possession would be placed in an expensive container. If this were the case, the container would be glorified instead of the treasure itself.

Today, you may think you have too many chips and cracks and fractures and fissures in your life to be used by God. Yet, as you acknowledge those imperfections, you are the perfect candidate to be used by God.

The stark contrast between the treasure and the earthen vessels that contain it is intended to show that transcendent power belongs to God and not to us. In 2 Corinthians 1:9, Paul testifies that the affliction he experienced in Asia taught him to "not rely on ourselves but on God, who raises the dead." And in a similar vein, the frailty of the messengers here demonstrates to the world that, in the words of C.G. Kruse, "the transcendent power belongs to God and not His envoys."[1]

Many people, like my friend Tray, are concerned about being seen in a favorable light by others. None of us desire to be looked upon as being

---

1   Kruse, C. G. (1987). *2 Corinthians: an introduction and commentary* (Vol. 8, pp. 106–107). Downers Grove, IL: InterVarsity Press.

worthless or insignificant, so we spend an inordinate amount of time and energy trying to validate and affirm who we are. Yet we neglect the reality that those who are proud, and are viewed well by others, are not those who God chooses to use for his work in the world. In fact, Paul assures us that God chooses to use a different type of person so that all of the glory will belong to Him!

God has demonstrated, through Paul's witness and testimony, that He is interested in using and blessing common, everyday people with noticeable imperfections to do extraordinary things. If you have everything together in your life, and have established yourself as the picture of perfection, you don't have a testimony of God's power and you've not given God much to work with! In the kingdom economy, God takes your brokenness and transforms it into a blessing. Not only *can* God use your damaged goods, God *wants* your damaged goods! It doesn't matter that others don't recognize your value or worth. God does. God has a history of using lives that are marred by circumstances for his glory. God is looking for individuals who don't care that their jars are leaky. The person who is open to being used by the Lord of All is the type of person God is looking to use and develop.

The Value of The Jar

Do you know the difference between an ordinary clay jar and an exotic expensive vase? To be honest, I didn't know until I began to research how much people are willing to spend for these expensive ornaments. Both vessels can be displayed as decorations. Both can hold flowers. Both can contain water. What makes the difference is the unique history of each vessel. For example, in a recent auction, the Chinese Qianlong vase set a new record as the most expensive porcelain item ever sold, when it was purchased for an unbelievable $53 million. The vase is from the 18th century and is approximately sixteen inches tall. It is decorated with images of fish and belonged to a royal family when it was taken during the Second Opium war. Steve Wynn purchased another vase for a donation to a public museum in Macau. This 600-year-old vase, engraved with red scrolling flowers, was sold for $10.1 million. I am sure there are many other pricy vases, but my point is that value is based on a *perception* of worth. This is not only true about collectables, but also applies to what we believe others think about us.

What people think about our jars matters to us more than we are typically willing to admit. It's pretty safe to say that all of us have been victims of trying to keep with up "Joneses." As a society, we spend an excessive amount of money and time trying to impress people we don't like and who don't like us. We focus on how good the jar looks to others instead of how our jars are being used.

Annually, Americans spend $55 billion on cosmetics, $13 billion on cosmetic surgery, $30 billion on athletic apparel, $60 billion on weight loss, and $90 billion on alcohol. These numbers astound me. They point to the effort, energy, and dollars we pour into trying to maintain the exterior of our jars. Namely, we're trying to preserve the illusion that our jars are not imperfect.

When we finally recognize and admit that they are broken, we finally realize that it was not enough to work on the exterior without investing in the interior. It is what's inside of us that creates our value. When your value is determined solely by your appearance, you eventually realize that you are not only externally broken but internally empty. What makes you valuable is not how well-kept your jar appears to others. Rather, it's what you possess on the inside that determines your value. You will discover that everyone may have a different opinion about the value of your jar but, ultimately, only God determines your value.

I have learned through my years of pastoral ministry that many people will harbor skewed perceptions about who you are when they don't even know you. They may even act like they are experts on you when they've not even met you. When it comes to your value, it is critical that your worth and value come from a source that is more reliable and unchanging than the opinions of your friends and acquaintances. When it comes to understanding your importance, your identity must come from a spring that is greater than your thirst.

It's an Inside Job

Human worth is not determined by a price tag someone else assigns, but by the Creator who made us! Many of us get discouraged by who and what we have become. We attempt to remedy our brokenness on our own instead of relying on the power that exceeds our human limitations. These attempts, to find our identity outside of God, lead to disappointment. Disappointments can lead to self-medication, as we attempt to mask our brokenness without ever experiencing the grace to move beyond our mistakes. Paul reminds us, "We have this treasure in jars of clay to show that this all-surpassing power is from God and not from us" (2 Cor. 4:7). This treasure that Paul refers to is revealed *through* our brokenness. Because of our faith and relationship with God, there is more within each of us than can be seen with the naked eye.

Our brokenness exposes God's power.

This treasure is revealed and seen through the fractured and shattered parts of our lives. It doesn't shine through us unless we've faced some broken moments in life. The path is not always a pretty one—there is heartache and disappointment and suffering along the way—but the cracks that are left in the wake of difficulty are where God's power can be seen and experienced. As a result, we can boldly speak the words of Paul: "We are hard-pressed on every side, but not crushed; perplexed, but not in despair; persecuted, but not abandoned; struck down, but not destroyed." It is the pressing on every side that makes a way for God's power to come through. Every difficult predicament makes space for the supernatural power of God to reside. We are not alone. And the harder we are hit, the stronger we rise.

Masterpiece

Have you ever had a conversation with yourself about what you are experiencing? Even though this might sound a little crazy, you begin the dialogue because you feel that what you are experiencing in life is unfair.

"Why do I have to go through this?"

"What is the purpose of this kind of pain?"

I want you to understand that God can use everything that happens in your life, whether it is tragic or triumphant, to bless you and grow you. I heard a friend of mine say, "God, wastes no wounds!" While you are going through difficult times, it may feel purposeless. But the very thing that almost broke you can become your greatest blessing! Remember the wounds you have experience were not wasted! God can turn a mess into a masterpiece! God takes master pieces and turns them into masterpieces!

Maybe you're experiencing a lot of stress and don't know how things will turn out for you. Maybe you've spent several years in ministry, and you thought by now you would see the fruit of your sacrifices, but you are still struggling to see your church grow. Maybe you are struggling with your child respecting you, and you feel helpless because everything that you have tried hasn't worked. You might feel like you've hit a wall and you can't push beyond the responsibility that you are carrying, but your boss is asking for more of you. Or maybe you want to retire but your healthcare needs mandate that you continue to work. I don't know what your situation is today, but God can use everything you are experiencing to demonstrate His power!

If you've lost both your parents...

If your daughter who's a straight-A college student comes home pregnant...

If your father or mother said you'd never amount to anything...

If you've experienced abuse or neglect...

...God's power can flow mightily through your cracked places!

My challenge to you is to choose how you view yourself in light of your brokenness. Choose to discover the beauty in the tapestry of the fragments of your life.

A New Day

Today is the day that you begin your journey to the next level. Are you excited? I am excited for you because I believe that you are about to tap into infinite possibilities. Your journey forward will require you to develop into a person that you have never known before. Yes, every "next level" will demand a different you! Are you ready? When you face this kind of possibility for transformation, you may wonder, "Why now?" or, "Why me?" My question to you is, "Why not you?" God created you, and that is enough reason to reach beyond where you are now to take the next steps to the place where God is leading you. The only thing standing between you and your next level is the story that you tell yourself about why you are not ready. This time, kill the story and begin the journey!

Lessons for You

There were so many lessons that we discovered in this chapter about brokenness.

My prayer is that you will begin your own journey toward exceptional purpose and start to practice these principles and apply them to your life. Use your personal hard knocks of life to develop into the person that God has destined you to become. Please consider these lessons for your journey:

- Your broken pieces have purpose!
- God can use fragments to create something that has never been before.
- When it comes to labels, speak life and not death.
- The power of life or death is in the tongue.
- What broke you does not have the final word. There is still room for God to mend the broken pieces.

- God's redemption of brokenness teaches us to never be judgmental toward others.

RECOGNIZE THIS

All of us have some level of brokenness within us.

DO THIS

- Make a decision to see a certified therapist to help you walk through the wounds of your past or present.

REFLECT ON THIS

- What are the past hurts that you have never dealt with that are hindering your progress today?

- What are some labels people have placed on you? Are they accurate?

- Do you think that the things people have said about you are true? Why or Why Not?

- In confronting your past troubles or pains, did you experience some level of healing?

- Can you find meaning in the current cracks and chips of your life?

CHAPTER 2

Broken from the Inside

"When the enemy cannot destroy you,
it is his job to distract you!"

—Author Unknown

I am still amazed that God chose to use me in spite of my background.

I didn't originate from a wealthy social or economic class, nor did I descend from a line of successful political figures, but God has used me anyway. God chose to use me—in spite of me!—and this keeps me grateful because I know that I am unworthy of the privileges that God has extended to me. I have been blessed to meet with dignitaries, the President of the United States of America, and other leaders who run the world. I want to encourage you that no matter where you came from, or how you started, nothing can keep you from experiencing the destiny God chose for your life. In the community where I was raised, on the Southside of Chicago, I learned early on about the importance of a strong desire, and drive, to live. If you don't have that desire, nothing in life will be given to you. In this world, only the most fit survive. If you want to live, you must learn how to survive. From my first day in school, and throughout the rest of my life, I was trained to survive.

Early on I was taught that, to get anything, I needed to earn it or fight for it. Those were the only two options. Thankfully, I later learned that this is not always the case if one encounters the grace of God! God will sometimes bless you with the very thing that you don't deserve. However, the world doesn't work that way. In the world you have to pursue what you want.

And along the way, you'll probably experience some bumps and bruises.

Unwilling to Back Down

I saw this during my senior of undergrad at Chicago State University. I was working full-time at Humana Health Care Plans, Inc. and was also a full-time student. Prior to this, I worked as a parking lot attendant. I parked cars from 11 pm to 7 am and would get off of work to attend school from 8 am to 1 pm, carrying a college schedule of twenty-one class hours. I maintained good grades while doing this, too. I was determined to finish school and I knew I had to work at the same time because I had no options for scholarships. There was no other choice. I made it to the finish line, and was ready to graduate, when I found out that there was a glitch in my transcript. I had completed all of my core courses with grades of B+ or higher, but that wasn't reflected on my transcripts.

There was one class where I'd been given the wrong grade. This grade caused all kinds of anxiety and stress because I knew I'd met the graduation requirements, but it felt like all of my efforts had been in vain. I appealed to the dean of my college, who did allow me to walk across the stage at graduation, but I still needed an accurate transcript. I was waiting to begin theological studies three months later, and I couldn't start school unless I had a complete transcript stating that I had graduated.

It was during this time that I learned to fight for what was rightfully mine! The grade had been an administrative error made by a visiting professor from Ghana who taught African American Studies. So I appealed to the Registrar's Office at Chicago State to change my grade. I had to resubmit all of my papers that I had completed from the class. Note to any student: save all of your work until you have completed the course and beyond! Keeping my classwork was my saving grace to prove that I'd done the work and had earned a B+.

However, the professor wasn't due to return to the university until the spring of the following year and this made it difficult for me to complete the grade change without him, since his signature was needed. My grade change issue became a battle that I didn't sign up to fight. I had completed all of my requirements to graduate, but the "powers that be" didn't want to assist me in changing my transcripts. This battle took place over the entire summer until, finally, I said to myself, "Enough is enough."

I went to Chicago State University on a hot steamy Monday morning in August with the determination that I was going to leave with my final transcripts in my hand. I remember it like it was yesterday. I sat in the Registrar's office for almost eight hours that day, hoping and praying that someone would help me. I was made to wait for this person and that person and I still never made any progress. No one was trying to help and, quite honestly, it felt like they didn't care.

Finally, I exclaimed to the director of the department, in a stern voice, "I need my transcripts, and I need them today!"

He stood there looking at me, without any care or compassion on his face, and said to me, "There is nothing that I can do."

I asked him, "Well, who has the authority to change my transcripts?"

Disinterested, he replied, "The President of the University can grant permission to change your records on the third floor, but you don't have clearance to see her."

This information was what I needed. I was determined, and his forbiddance was my marching orders to fight for myself. Having nothing to lose, I climbed the stairs to the third floor and asked to speak to the President. During my four and half years as a student there I had never been to the President's office. I was nervous, but determined to get justice. And my transcripts.

To my surprise, the person at the desk was a lady I'd served with, as an intern, during my freshmen year, and the acting President was my former freshman year counselor. You never know when those relationships will come in handy! I told them everything that happened to me, and I pleaded my case to the President. The President made one call, and the staff in the Registrar's office immediately started to work on my behalf. People who were ready to go home at the end of the day had to work overtime until my transcripts were changed. As a result, I was able to start seminary on time.

This experience taught me a treasured lesson: Never give up—it doesn't matter how many "no's" you receive; you only need one "yes." I learned that you must be willing to fight for yourself even when the odds are stacked against you. When life seems unfair, you must purpose to never give up. Battles can make you stronger. As you fight them, you are gaining strength.

Called to an Imperfect Church

The next chapter in my life had some similar experiences. During this season, the Bishop encouraged me to quit my job with Humana so that I could begin my full-time pastoral ministry while I was still a full-time seminary student.

I was ready for that next step, but it was one of the scariest experience in my life! Full of blind faith at twenty-one, I left a job that was paying $60,000 a year to serve as a pastor. When I started I was making $375.00 a week. Less than four-hundred dollars a week to support a new family. Wow. I still can't believe I did that. I had to move about an hour away from where I lived to a town northeast of Chicago called Evanston, known for being the home of Northwestern University and for having an active Methodist heritage. It was also the home of Garrett-Evangelical Theological Seminary. The Bishop assigned me to serve a small church called New Hope CME (Christian Methodist Episcopal) Church, located on Grey Avenue. The parsonage, where the pastor's family lived, was located on Church Street.

When I was appointed to New Hope CME Church, I was one of the youngest pastors to ever serve the church. The congregation immediately let me know that they had trained many pastors before me, and that they would do the same for me. Many of their former pastors became Bishops in the church, and they were proud to have a hand in shaping the leadership of the connectional church.

Unfortunately, although the church had a rich heritage, it also had a culture where they fought all of the time. I mean *all of the time*. I wasn't used to this and hadn't signed up to continue the tradition. I was being trained in conflict and knew I was at risk of imitating some of their bad habits! The culture of conflict I'd walked into had sprung from brokenness.

A week after I'd arrived, I performed a funeral, and eulogy, for the son of a family in the congregation. I wanted to make the tribute personal and meaningful for the family. When the day of the funeral arrived, I'd still not heard anyone mention his name. I was preparing to stand to preach before this new body, including many members who I had never seen before. I was anxious, but confident that I'd prepared appropriately. As I was standing up preaching, I used the name of the deceased young man several times.

After the third or fourth time that I said "Darren" in my message, a lady hollered out in the middle of the service, "His name is Darryl!"

Embarrassed, I felt like I was in a Southwest Airlines commercial because "I wanted to get away." All I could do was keep preaching and, in the middle of the message, apologize and ask forgiveness. I was able to get through that moment, but it will remain with me for the rest of my life. As I reflect on it now, it's a little funny. But it wasn't funny then!

I won't lie, that was one of the rougher moments in my pastoral ministry. I wanted more than anything to establish my leadership and to let these folks know that I cared about them. And I didn't know if it would take weeks or years to regain the trust and influence that had been lost in that fateful syllable.

It was hard to see how God was going to use my brokenness for good.

Function in Dysfunction

This church had learned, as I like to say, to "function in dysfunction." For example, they were used to having clashes in church conference, but I refused to engage in their fight. While serving there, I experienced the threat of a church split, a change of lay leadership due to death, and people withholding funds because they didn't like some of the decisions that I'd made. I was being baptized by fire in the pastoral waters of church conflict management, and the only thing I desired was to be a good pastor. I would call more experienced pastors for advice, but what they shared didn't ever seem to work for me. Desperate, I started to pray like never before. I asked God to reveal me what I should do and how I should do it. This church was indeed training me, as they'd promised, but it wasn't what I had in mind! In spite of it all, the Lord blessed our church, and even blessed my family, during my tenure at New Hope. We grew from about forty-one members in attendance to over one hundred worshippers every Sunday. I was gradually discovering my gifts as a preacher, teacher, and leader in ministry. Some of my fondest memories are knit into the fabric of this church, and I will forever cherish its impact on my life.

Maybe you've had a season like this one, where you faced more challenges than you'd bargained for. Maybe the folks you thought had your back were actually conspiring against you behind your back! Though it can feel like God has abandoned you during these times, God's power is actually seen most clearly in the broken and bruised parts of our lives.

David and Saul

After serving at New Hope, God sent me to another congregation in Evanston where I was able to discover and use many of the gifts and skills for ministry that I'd not yet tapped. I was on loan to the Mt. Zion Church and was excited about the possibilities there. Mt. Zion was a pivotal part of my development and it was also the place where I *really* learned to trust in God. It also gave me a better sense of why God had called me in the first place. This pastoral assignment was my opportunity to prove my commitment to pastoral ministry and also a chance for my gifts for ministry to be validated in a new environment.

I'd been courted to work at this iconic community church for two years. Finally, I felt God calling me to do so. Believing God was calling me to this place, I jumped in head first to this new assignment! Thankfully, I had a mentor to guide me. I'll call him Dr. Henderson. He was a well-known and revered leader in Evanston, with a rich history of service to the community and the church. When I arrived at Mt. Zion, Dr. Henderson—who'd also served Mt. Zion—took me under his wing.

One of my first projects at Mt. Zion was to design both a Bible study curriculum and a prayer meeting. At that time the church didn't have an active Bible study or a corporate prayer ministry. So I had the opportunity to create a foundation for the spiritual nurture and growth of our members. Within two weeks of the launch of the prayer meeting and the Bible study, we had over two hundred people in attendance at each ministry event. The church members were excited that I was there, and things were feeling great. I knew, beyond a shadow of a doubt, that this was the place God wanted me to serve.

Though I was winning with the people, I soon discovered that I was losing with my mentor. I hadn't seen that coming. Early on, he'd begun criticizing everything that I presented and produced. Regularly, my contributions were being discredited. I knew God had called me to be a pastor, though, because it wasn't something that I wanted or even dreamed of ever doing. I'd planned to practice medicine and become an anesthesiologist. So all of this criticism came as a shock. I couldn't believe some of the comments coming from one who'd admired me enough to bring me on board. All I could do was to try to do the work I'd been called to do as faithfully as I could do it. I worked long hours, sometimes twelve to fourteen hours a day, just to prove that I was fit for the position. I quickly discovered, though, that no matter how hard I tried, I wouldn't receive his affirmation.

Against my will, my mentor and I established a David and Saul relationship. David, before he became king, was a son of a shepherd. David famously destroyed the giant Goliath and, in the wake of that amazing victory, this shepherd's boy became extremely popular among the people. The more well-known David became, the more jealous and envious King Saul became. Before this turn in their relationship, David had ministered to Saul by playing his harp for the king and offering Saul relief from his suffering. David had always had a good rapport with Saul, and they'd always respected each other. But the relationship went south because Saul's ego couldn't handle David's success. Lisa Bevere, author of *Girls With Swords: How to Carry Your Cross Like a Hero*, traces the rocky relationship between the two men. She observes that David had navigated being misrepresented to Saul, then misrepresented by Saul, then chased by Saul, and forgiven by Saul, only to be misrepresented yet again, and then chased once again by Saul, from cave to cave, and from hiding place to hiding place. No matter what David did, even when he remained loyal, it wasn't enough to please Saul.

The odd shift in my relationship with the mentor I'd trusted triggered a similar pain. I felt like I was being chased by the person who should have been my guide. I discovered that he'd lied about the compensation package that I was to receive. That was just one piece in a puzzle revealing a picture in which he was trying to prove that his leadership was still significant in the life of the congregation.

During January of my first year at the church, I was waiting for the healthcare coverage that had been promised when I was offered the position. Yet I kept being put off until I finally spoke up in a meeting with the treasurer and Dr. Henderson, desperate to know the status of my health insurance. The coverage was crucial because my daughter was about to be born and we couldn't afford the medical bills without that coverage.

In front of the treasurer, Dr. Henderson stated bluntly, "I can't give it to you."

He gave no explanation.

I was devastated, angry, and felt disrespected. I had to find some other way to provide the health coverage that my family so desperately needed, but I knew this wasn't the time to quit.

My first instinct was to pull out my sword and fight the way I was trained to fight. I *knew* how to win with a sword. But the Spirit didn't release me to use my scrappy fighting skills in this battle. Over the next two years, the twists and turns of this sticky relationship continued to manifest. I knew I needed to use a different tool if I was going to survive and thrive. My sword wasn't sufficient for this battle, despite the deep desire of my heart to slay a menacing giant with force.

Maybe you've faced giants of your own. An exacting boss. An abusive partner. A sibling who bullied. A self-serving pastor. You know the influence these giants can have on your life, and how they can trigger the widening of fissures in your heart.

Am I enough?

Do I have what it takes?

Maybe he's right...

Maybe it is my fault...

When a menacing personality triggers those cracks inside you, it can be tempting to either surrender or to grab your sword. But there's another way.

The Tool God Wanted Me to Use

I eventually discovered that, as long as I was in this relationship, I'd be miserable if I didn't learn how to do something differently. Thankfully, God showed me what tool I should use.

During the season of my one-year anniversary, the congregation gave me a pastoral appreciation weekend with a worship service and dinner event. I invited my home church pastor, Rev. Jerome B. Price Sr., to preach for me. I was excited for the congregation to meet Reverend Price and was looking forward to a great weekend. My appreciation weekend was scheduled for one late-spring weekend, but without consulting me, the date of the celebration was changed. A leader in the church told me, quietly and privately, that the juggling was an intentional effort to force to me give up and quit. The new date for the "appreciation" was Memorial Day weekend when most of the people in the church were scheduled to be traveling. My only response was to pray for guidance and direction. As I prayed, God revealed to me how I was to respond. During prayer time God gave me a vision of the new tool that I should use; it was a staff! With His signature, gentle leading, God reminded that He didn't call me to be a warrior but to be a *shepherd* who led his sheep.

According to John W. Ritenbaugh, in biblical days, the staff was used in three ways.[1]

First, the staff is used to draw sheep together. This is particularly important when many lambs are being born. The shepherd has to make sure the right lamb stays with the right ewe. If there's any question about which lamb belongs with which ewe, the shepherd picks the lamb up with his staff, and carries it to the proper ewe. He cannot touch the lamb. If he touches the lamb, the ewe will not suckle it because of the foreign odor that the ewe fears: the smell of the human. The ewe will refuse to feed her young.

Secondly, the staff is used to reach out and harness a lamb for close inspection. If the shepherd needs to check a lamb for blemish or injury, he uses his staff.

Finally, the staff is used to corral sheep that stray from the flock. Poking the sheep in the ribs, he'll guide it back toward the flock.

Ritenbaugh's explanation unpacks why this particular tool would be so important for my journey. My purpose wasn't to fight with Saul. My purpose was to shepherd the sheep that were assigned to me in that season.

And God was faithful to provide the tool I needed to do that. During that difficult season, I learned that God always intercedes before we are forced to abort the work God is birthing through us! David was anointed to be a shepherd and not a murderer. I was anointed to be a pastor, so God called me to switch tools, laying down my sword and picking up His staff.

And guess what happened? That weekend, which was orchestrated to be anticlimactic and disappointing, became one of the best ones I experienced during my early ministry. Folks in the church chose to stay home instead of traveling out of town. In fact, the house was packed. And just when I thought my presence wasn't wanted, I was affirmed both by God's grace and also by the love of the people. It is always interesting how God will use a broken moment to confirm our truest identities.

During that rocky period, I didn't know who to trust because everybody that was *by* my side wasn't necessary *on* my side. When the rift in the relationship with my mentor became evident, other ministers began to vie for position and power. I discovered the hard way that the church can be very political. As a result of that season, I learned to discern those who had my best interest at heart. I was intentional about building relationships with the people God had assigned to cover me during that trying time.

The tool I used was the shepherd's staff. I tried to help people learn to draw close and love one another. I guided people to hear God's voice by studying his Word. I led them to cry out to God by praying together. It wasn't a sword, but a staff that God handed me so that I could fulfill my assignment with faithfulness and integrity.

Broken

The people began to pray for me, but as the days grew in tenure, it became harder to stay. I was grateful that others saw my worth, but, for the first time in my ministry, I was fractured. I was broken on the inside. How could I move forward and believe that I hadn't made a mistake about the opportunity and the assignment? It was clear that I had the peace of God to move forward, but it wasn't clear to why I needed to go through the grueling process.

God later revealed to me that this wasn't about where I'd been planted, but it was about what God had placed in me. God had anointed me to preach, teach, pastor, and grow His kingdom. And although I'd been able to do those things, I was still broken by the painful experience. Yet I could see that God was teaching me not to trust another human being with my destiny, but always to rely on the hand of God to guide my steps.

Trusting God allowed me to be grateful for all of the tools God had given me through that particular ministry. I became a better administrator, steward, preacher, and leader as a result. I'd definitely been called to go to Mt. Zion, but not meant to stay. I remember clearly my last Sunday there. I arrived at the church around seven that morning because I needed to pray. Serving there had become almost unbearable and I had nowhere else to turn.

"Lord," I begged, "I can't take this anymore."

Little did I know that morning that it would be my last Sunday at Mt. Zion.

That season was my "rite of passage" into pastoral leadership and into adulthood. Honestly, I credit that experience at Mt. Zion as the chrysalis for the growth that trained me to become effective in ministry! In a chrysalis, a tender caterpillar undergoes a metamorphosis to become a colorful butterfly. It's a painful but necessary process for the caterpillar to transform into what God intended for it to be. I needed this process to become what God intended for me. Specifically, I had to endure brokenness to become the man and the leader I am today. Though I couldn't see it at the time, God exchanged the embarrassment, rejection, betrayal, and abandonment I endured for the purpose He continues to reveal.

Maybe you've also been bruised and broken by trying experiences that you never would have chosen for yourself. If that's where you've been, or if that's where you are today, I can assure you that you are not alone. God's power is made manifest through your broken places. When you're pressed on every side, it can feel as though you will be crushed. But I can report that, although some of these experiences feel death-dealing at the time, they will not destroy you.

They cannot, because the power of God is alive in you.

Next Steps

Things didn't end well for me at Mt. Zion. After being given a check for three months' salary, I was relieved to leave. Folks in the church encouraged me to fight and wait, but I knew my season was over, and it was time for me to move forward. Today I am grateful for the lessons I learned and even for the challenges that forced me to grow as a man and as an effectual servant. The best part of it all was that, because of what I'd endured, I knew I could serve effectively in ministry in any context. That was, and continues to be, a blessing to me.

I am grateful for the patience of Bishop Isom, who allowed me to discover my gifts on the journey. During that transitory season, friends invited me to preach for them almost every Sunday until I saw clearly what God's next steps for me would be. I am grateful for friends like Bishop Marvin Frank Thomas, Rev. Kenneth Cherry, and Dr. L. Bernard Jakes, who walked with me through the valley of the shadow of death. By sharing their pulpits, they allowed me to continue to exercise my gifts and feel the presence of God's Holy Spirit comforting me when I most needed it.

One day, one of the mothers of my home church called me and issued a directive to return to the place that knew my worth and value. Mrs. Zelda Q. Birdsong became my angel who called Bishops to intercede on my behalf. I received several offers of appointments to serve locally, but God didn't release me to consider any of them. It wasn't until I began conversations with the newly-elected Bishop Henry M. Williamson Sr. that my story changed.

I could not have imagined what God had in store.

Lessons for You

I hope you're able to learn and grow from the painful lessons I learned during this season of my life. My prayer is that you are able to avoid some situations that I didn't. Though I don't wish those fiery trials upon you, I do believe that, by God's grace, they can mold you into a more effective person and leader.

- Do your research before you select your mentors—or before they select you! Understand their story before you allow them to begin to write yours.

- If you've already made the wrong choice, admit it and move on!

- Listen to those who have covering over your life, those who are responsible for your success and growth as a person.

- What you internalize can determine what you will actualize. Have conviction and clarity about your purpose. If you don't, others will begin to speak untrue words into your life that begin to define who you are.

- The rejection that you felt and experienced wasn't meant to *define* you but to *refine* you! Had you not been rejected you would not have honed your skills. Had they not closed the door on your face, you wouldn't have built your door!

- Doing the right thing doesn't always lead to a Hollywood ending.

RECOGNIZE THIS

Choose to allow others' critiques to sharpen you but not define you.

DO THIS

Remember those who've affirmed you. When God gives you success and favor, don't forget to bless them, thank them, and also give them a copy of this book!

REFLECT ON THIS

- When have you recognized that you have made a mistake? How did you change course?

- What have you learned from a difficult situation in your own life?

- Who affirmed you when you doubted your gifts or God's purpose for your life? Was that man or woman a seasonal person in your life or someone who remains a constant part of your life?

- The sharpening process can be rough. What are experiences that you didn't enjoy, but that eventually made you better?

- What did you learn about yourself in this process?

- What new gifts emerged as a result of your sharpening process?

CHAPTER 3

Shattered Pieces

"When it seems that someone
has shattered your dreams . . .
Pick up even the smallest pieces and
use them to build bigger
and better dreams."
–Jeremy Irons

Bishop Henry M. Williamson, Sr., served my home church, St. Paul CME, as an assistant pastor. We had a strong history together since he watched me develop into a young minister. He served as senior pastor for sixteen years at Carter Temple CME Church, Chicago, and served in various capacities within the annual conference.

When I was waiting on God's next assignment for me, Bishop Williamson invited me to visit his Chicago office, at 79th and Wabash, to discuss my future.

Our conversation would change the course of my ministry and my life.

Though I'd heard stories of pastors packing up their belongings and setting out across the country with their families to serve God, the possibility seemed like something out of a storybook rather than a real possibility for my family and me. (Honestly, it seemed like God's call to Abram!) In fact, when the Bishop threw out the idea of serving a church on the West Coast, I had no desire at all to go. Born, raised, and educated in Chicago, it felt a little scary to imagine setting down roots so far from home.

There were no commitments made that day, just a suggestion of the possibility of the church making room for me. Most importantly, it was an opportunity for me to serve as a pastor under the Bishop's leadership. As the meeting came to a close, he said words that rang in my ears like the sound of the elementary school bell ringing when class was dismissed.

As he ushered me to the door and out into the hallway, he chimed, "I will call you in two weeks, and when I do I will tell you, 'Go west young man, go west!'"

Leaving his office and driving back to my home in Evanston was a longer drive than I'd ever remembered it being. I called my family to discuss the possibility of moving west together.

I had lived in Chicago my entire life, and I knew nothing about California. If I didn't receive the call, or decided not go, what would my life look like? How could I remain faithful to God's call on my life? I was more convinced than ever that I was called to pastor and guide individuals into a meaningful relationship with God, but I had to deal with my fears about how I should fulfill this calling that God had given me. It had simply never before crossed my mind that ministry for me could be outside of the state lines of Illinois! So in those early hours and days, I didn't have peace about the possibility of moving. Every time the subject of moving would come up my mouth would become parched. My back would tense up, and my thoughts would bounce around my mind. I had the audacity to say that God had called me to preach and pastor, and even that I'd go where He led me, but moving across the country tested my faith at another level. Wanting nothing more than to obey God's voice, I asked for peace so that I'd be ready when the call came.

One late afternoon I decided to take a drive to Northwestern University. I was familiar with the campus as I'd spent many days walking the banks of Lake Michigan to give me solace in the midst of my studies at Garrett-Evangelical Theological Seminary. Those evening strolls were moments of relief from a challenging class load and intense study. But this time it was about making one of the most difficult decisions in my life. I sat crouched on rocks that decorated the ends of the lake. I watched as people jogged by and also noticed as others sat on the shore as if they, like me, were carrying heavy burdens. The afternoon rolled into evening as if God himself was pulling down the shade of night to cover the day's brightness. The waves were rolling in as the tide rose, and I began to pray to God for direction and wisdom.

I needed God to show me that it was okay to leave Chicago and, if that was God's will, to equip me to let go of all that was familiar.

In the midst of this, I remembered the words of my mother. "Watch the waves when you pray," she'd told me. "Take every worry that is in your heart and allow the waves to carry each one away."

It was at that moment that I began to mentally place every struggle that I carried and every concern that I harbored on the waves rolling into the shore. One by one, my worries started to drift away.

I could finally hear God speaking in a clear voice to me declaring, "It's okay."

This was a kairos moment for me as I was able to pick up the broken pieces and find the strength and peace to reassemble the dream that God had spoken into my life years earlier. Though I'd assumed that the broken shards of experience were beyond repair, I saw God begin to piece them back into a functional whole.

When I returned home that evening, I began sharing with my family the peace that I had and the excitement and anticipation about trusting God in a way I hadn't experienced before. I reminded them of the Scriptures when God called Abram to leave his familiar home to go to a foreign land. Genesis proclaims, "The Lord had said to Abram, 'Go from your country, your people and your father's household to the land I will show you' (Gen. 12:1). Buoyed by trust in God's reliability, Abram was obedient to the call.

This obedience is critical to embracing God's purpose for your life before launching out into deep waters of faith.

The Call

Developing your relationship with the Lord requires trusting God with your life.

I was at peace with trusting *God* with my life, but the next level of trusting God was to believe in Bishop Williamson for godly judgment. Trusting those God has appointed is fairly palatable when you're in familiar territory—aka your "comfort zone"—but it becomes a thriller when you have no idea where you are being sent!

I received "the call" from the Bishop with explicit instructions: "I need you to purchase your ticket and come to Southern California."

Now, let me say that before I received this call, the devil had been busy.

In fact, as if the devil had ordered a mass-assault on my already shattered faith, I received a number of other calls from people with less godly judgment than the Bishop. If I listened to them, I'd have agreed to a number of pastorates to which I'd not been called. I had to stop listening to the chatter of these voices and keep preparing to receive the call God had for me.

This lesson is essential for you to understand. When you're going through a season in which you've been shattered, it is critical that you place people on mute who don't have a say in your future. If they are not decision makers, they are distractors to your destiny. Listen only to those who have your best interest at your heart.

I bought my ticket and flew to the Southern California Region Annual Conference. Many of my childhood friends were there waiting to receive appointments from the newly minted Presiding Bishop. I was scheduled to preach at the meeting, and was nervous about how others would react to my style and persona as a preacher. I'm never worried during the act of preaching, because I know God has called me, but as I prepared to preach

I was concerned that the leaders in the denomination might not like or receive me. This became yet another opportunity to pray for God's peace. Thankfully, the preaching moment unfolded just like I was at home. And although the people at the conference received me with open arms, the worst of my fears were not over.

After preaching on Tuesday, I had a couple more days before hearing the reading of the appointments. In the Methodist church tradition, the presiding bishops announce the assignments where pastors will be serving the following year. The reading of the pastoral appointments was a tense time because we had no idea where we'd been assigned. At least this was my story.

Friday morning I was sitting in the audience, waiting for the Bishop to read my name.

"Rev. Charley Hames Jr...."

I held my breath.

"...Curry Temple CME Church. Compton, California."

What?!?

Compton, like the neighborhood where rappers Easy E, Ice Cube and NWA lived?!

Everything I had heard about Compton was bad, and now I'd been called to serve there as a pastor.

Since I'd grown up on the Southside of Chicago, I tried to convince myself there was no reason to be scared. After my appointment had been announced, I began to meet a few of the church members who attended the conference. It began to seem like things would be okay, as long as I had a bulletproof pulpit. I met an elderly lady who was the administrative assistant at the church.

She greeted me with a huge smile and said, "Hi Pastor, I am your secretary if you choose to still have me."

Her warmth melted my heart.

"Absolutely," I confirmed. "I won't be able to do it without you."

I met a few more who appeared skeptical of me. I immediately felt a distance from them. I thought this was odd because we'd just met. What was the vibe I was getting? But I knew not react to my perception, which may or may not be accurate.

I went back to my hotel room, exhausted from the day, to hold a meeting with one of my new leaders.

My colleagues were out celebrating their new appointments with the Bishop while I met with the financial officer of my new church. I welcomed him into my room, and for about forty-five minutes he filled me in on the state of the church's financial affairs. And it was *not pretty*. The room actually seemed to grow darker as he spoke. Eventually I felt so desperate that I politely asked him to leave. This was clearly a shattered church, damaged by mismanagement and poor decisions, and I'd just met with a broken leader. As reality began to set in, I realized how difficult my new appointment could be. I was a broken pastor, who'd just left a broken church, entering into another. Feeling like God had allowed this to happen again, my initial reaction was anger.

How do you respond when life leaves you feeling broken?

What do you when circumstances cause you to feel defeated and crushed?

At the time, I had no idea how to play the hand I'd been dealt. Especially since God and I were not on good terms. My reaction wasn't holy and what came pouring out of my mouth wasn't, "Thank you, Jesus."

In the midst of my rant, I heard God say, as plain as day, "Shut up!"

Humbled, I realized that I had no idea what the Lord Almighty was up to in my life.

Gradually I realized that, not only was God not done with me, God wasn't done with Curry Temple.

That night, when I returned from the conference, I learned that Curry Temple didn't have a church building. For twelve years, they'd attempted to build one, but it didn't happen. I heard, in the stories church members shared; stories of brokenness. They didn't own a pastor's residence and their resources were zero. In fact, the financial officer shared with me that the church had three accounts: two of them were at zero, and the third account was a negative $247! So we would have to pay the bank back before we could start doing business there again. The congregation was renting an AME Zion church for Sunday worship services, with no new home in sight. The majority of the members had left, and those who remained were feeling unproductive, unfruitful, crushed, and forgotten by God.

I wasn't the only one who had questions about God's faithfulness.

The Preaching Moment

I arrived at Martin Temple AME Zion Church the day after the conference to preach for the Curry Temple congregation. I wasn't sure how things would go.

As I got out of the car, the sun was shining bright and I could smell the dew that blanketed the grass.

I was discovering that Compton was more than the backdrop for videos from my favorite rappers. It was a city that had seen a lot of change over the previous decades. And it was largely populated by Hispanic families and African American families who'd refused to move out because of their love for the city.

Walking into the church, I felt a sweet spirit of hope that permeated our temporary dwelling as the members of Curry Temple gathered to worship! Forty-two people showed up for my first service. I preached and I felt God's faithful hand with me that day.

I met with church leaders the Monday morning after that first worship service. Together we made a commitment to trust each other because we had no other choice. I made a promise to them that I would remain transparent, responsible, and accountable as their pastor. What I needed in return was the very thing that they gave their previous leaders: trust and a willingness to follow. The next Sunday was the first Sunday since we'd decided together to pick up the pieces of our shattered dreams.

I dreamed of being an effective pastor by growing a healthy and thriving church. The people of Curry Temple dreamed of walking into their new church building one day. We knew and understood that if our dreams were to become a reality, we both had to offer our broken pieces and allow God to make us whole again. The next season wouldn't be easy, but those days were the most memorable of my life. God used the hard knocks of Compton, California to develop me into the leader I was supposed to become.

A poem by Toni Umbrace captures that experience for me:

> Broken lives You've placed before me
> Shattered pieces scattered 'roun
> Directly in my path, they've fallen
> This path that You have led me down.
> How many times have I, neglectful
> Stepped over, turned or walked around
> Those pieces meant to be my burden
> Who lost, were longing to be found?

Staying in the Preacher's House and One-Way Tickets

I was moving to serve a church that didn't have housing for the pastor and also didn't have enough resources to rent a place for us at that time. In the midst of all of this, when the church couldn't afford to put me up in a hotel, there was a preacher who offered his home to me while I served my first days in the city of Compton. The home of Rev. Joseph Gardner became my home, and I will never forget this.

After that Sunday, I tried to learn more about the work that had been started by the previous pastor and tried to see what the potential could be for the new church.

That week a group of us visited the campus of the new church site. We were welcomed by a graffiti-tagged building with unkempt grounds that spanned as far as your eyes could see. I stood beside Bishop Williamson, Rev. J.J. Jackson, Rev. Peris Lester, and Will, who'd driven us there. We all stood speechless in front of the run-down property. We carefully walked onto the unpaved site and climbed the embankment, where the driveway should have been, to be able to see the structure of the church. When the congregation ran out of resources to finish the work, the church was about two-thirds complete. This meant the walls were up, the roof had been framed, but there was no drywall, windows, or roof shingles. It was a shell of what we hoped was to come.

We walked into the gray stucco structure that was filled with dust and debris. As we walked, silence filled the room. I felt like we were walking through the valley of the shadow of death. We were stopped in our tracks as we faced two tons of garbage that sat in the middle of the future sanctuary.

My eyes grew dim and a voice in my head said, "There ain't no way in hell you are going to finish this church in ninety days—or ninety years, for that matter."

Before another negative thought could force its way into my mind, Bishop Williamson's raspy voice echoed through the walls of the future sanctuary.

He bellowed, "Son, oh yeah! You can do this!"

He kept repeating these words until those who were with us began to repeat them with him.

With a prophetic tone, Bishop Williamson began to speak what I was not yet able to see in myself: "It's in you, and I believe you can do this. There is no doubt in my mind that it shall come to pass!"

After we prayed that day, the drive that I needed began to manifest itself. On that day, I learned the meaning of the words penned by an unknown author, "When God leads you to the edge of the cliff, trust Him fully and let go. Only one of two things will happen: either He'll catch you when you fall, or He'll teach you how to fly!"

Go West

The next day, I went back to Evanston to sell my home and prepare to move my family back to California. It was a ten-day turnaround in which we had to sign the papers, pack and move two little boys and a newborn girl across the country to our new assignment. This time was filled with excitement, grief, and anticipation all at once.

But the congregation had still not able to raise sufficient funds to cover the salary package.

I bought one-way tickets on Southwest Airlines to be in California that Saturday for Sunday worship. This time was tough because my best friend from childhood lost his mother and I couldn't attend the funeral because my tickets were non-refundable, and I didn't yet know where my family would live once we arrived. This unfortunate moment severed our relationship because he couldn't understand why I couldn't be present. I regretted it desperately, but I was in a terrible position.

When I returned with my family, there wasn't enough space for all of us to stay with Reverend Gardner, so we stayed at a member's house in Los Angeles until we could figure out our housing situation. These times were very stressful because I'd moved my family two thousand miles from their familiar surroundings to be homeless. We stayed in the home of Ms. May for a couple of weeks until we held a church conference about my housing allowance.

Little did I know that the lady who had offered to be my administrative assistant on the day I'd received my assignment would end up being my guardian angel. Mother Nelda Faye Lakey-Woods was adamant that I needed a house for my family. So, on the night of the church conference, she presented information about a house that a group of members had researched on our behalf.

She said to those gathered, "Now listen, I know we haven't done much in the past, but I believe in our pastor, and we will raise the money needed to provide for his family as he helps us build our church. We are going to do it, and there is nothing else to be said."

I looked around the room, and was relieved to see that no one was either fighting back or walking out.

She added, "I believe that if we take care of Pastor, he will take care of us!"

The room was dead silent.

Then one member began to affirm her statements. Then another agreed, until the entire membership was on board. Mother Lakey-Woods, who was suffering a terminal illness, added that she wanted to walk through those doors of her church before she died.

I was seeing God's power flowing through those who, like me, were broken vessels.

We'd moved into a home in Carson, California, and people started to help in ways that I couldn't imagine. The salary was small, only $500 a week, to provide for a family of five, including a newborn. To make ends meet, we lived off our savings for the first couple of months of my assignment as pastor. I would be on the site of the new church from seven in the morning until ten at night, making sure the contractors would show up and keep the project moving forward. One church member would come faithfully to our house every week and fill our refrigerator with food so that we didn't have worry about groceries. We didn't have much, but God was more than enough and this church that had been shattered by life was starting to heal in ways that I couldn't imagine.

I was healing too.

Ninety Days

When I'd been appointed, Bishop Williamson challenged me to complete Curry Temple within ninety days of my new assignment. The challenge was absurd. All the odds were stacked against us. We had a dwindling membership, no financial resources, and a shady contractor who had no desire to finish this project. I spent days and nights at the site of the new church: watching over sub-contractors, holding the foreman accountable, and making sure the building was passing inspections for all of the city codes. Somehow, by God's grace, we came through it all. Curry Temple began to raise money like never before. We raised record numbers of funds to continue the unfinished work while paying a mortgage in excess of $4,000 a month. One of the blessings of being a part of a connectional church is that there are resources beyond your congregation to be utilized. We were able to call in members of our sister churches to lay the carpet, as well as offer other items that were needed to build and open a church.

I believe what helped our broken pieces join together to form a more complete whole was our active prayer life. Every week, during the middle of the day, we walked around that building site seven times, just as Joshua and the children of Israel marched around the walls of Jericho. We would circle the pile of garbage praying that God would change our situation and turn things around. We were consistent in prayer every week, for sixteen weeks, until the middle of December. Week by week, the garbage began to disappear, the graffiti on the wall was covered, the drywall was installed, and the building started to become a church. As we were building the pulpit, I requested that the contractor put a Bible in the floor, in front of the pulpit. I wanted every preacher who would preach in this church to be standing on the word of God. God was building Curry Temple through the sacrifice of the congregation, and we would soon walk into our new home.

The ninety days had come and gone, and Bishop Williamson was preparing for his Mid-Winter Conference, scheduled to be held at the new Curry Temple CME Church. The morning of the service, everything was almost complete, except that the carpet wasn't laid, the pews weren't installed, and the electricity wasn't on! To make matters worse, he brought Bishop Isom by that morning to see everything. I was sweating bullets. I believed it was going to be ready, but I didn't necessarily know when. So I started to use the words on him that he used on me.

"Oh yes, Bishop it's going to happen!"

Bishop Isom cracked a joke on me and said, "Son, I heard Jesus turned water into wine, and he took two fish and five barley loaves and fed five thousand."

I liked where this was heading.

Then he said, "Guess what, son?"

"What sir?" I answered.

Grinning, he teased, "You ain't Jesus!"

Looking around at the challenge before me, I breathed a silent prayer of desperation, "Jesus be a carpenter! I need you now!"

The Extension Cord

God always comes through when you need Him the most. This is my testimony and I'm sticking by it!

On the opening day of Mid-Winter Conference, our congregation and the entire conference walked through the doors of Curry Temple! People were excited for the great things God had done through our hard work, persistence, and prayers. The church was complete, for the most part, and we were granted temporary occupancy through the city of Compton for ninety days until we gained a permanent certificate of occupancy.

However, there was one obstacle we'd not been able to scale. We had no electricity for that night or for future services. Though the city wouldn't grant us the right to turn on the power, the foreman was able to take the temporary power pole and connect power to the building through an extension cord. I shout every time I think about this modern-day miracle. Though we didn't have access to the main power source, we used a heavy-duty extension cord to connect to the power. On our own, we don't have the authority, but God works even in our brokenness to connect us to the power source.

Curry Temple had a stellar moment in faith and ministry during that year! We grew from forty-two members to over 350 by the end of the year. There was love in that congregation like never before. Members were sharing their faith in amazing ways, and the church fellowship was the happiest it had been in years. There were even more miracle stories that happened that year than I can share here. God was able to take a shattered leader, leading a shattered people, and mend us in ways we could not have imagined. Curry Temple finally gained permanent occupancy that year, and it is still serving the Compton community today. Although I couldn't have imagined how God would restore the wreckage of my life, or that church, this story stands a testament that finding favor is possible in the midst of the broken pieces of your life.

Maybe, against your will, your family has been shattered by tragedy, death, divorce, or abandonment. Maybe you or a loved one is facing an illness today, and you can't even imagine how God can reassemble the pieces of your lives. Maybe you've faced a financial crisis that has left you broken and scared.

Beloved, I am confident that God has not abandoned you. When we are at our weakest, God is at His strongest.

I know what it's like to feel that God doesn't have your back. Believe me, I get it. But I can testify that God can do more than you can hope or imagine with the broken pieces of your life.

Offer them to Him today, and see what happens.

Lessons for You

I pray that, as you look at your shattered pieces, God will begin to reassemble them for His glory. As you offer those pieces to God, your personal hard knocks can be used to develop you into the person that God has destined you to become. Please consider these lessons for your journey:

- Come to every situation with an open mind.
- When you are placed in a desperate situation, there is no other place to turn but to God.
- In the course of time, God will answer your prayers.
- God is not obligated to respond to your request, but He has the right to accept your offer.
- We are not called to bargain with God, but we are called to trust Him.

- It may seem like life has left you for dead, but if you continue the course God will remember you!

RECOGNIZE THIS

Every adversity is an opportunity for his divine affirmation!

DO THIS

Don't misjudge your opportunity as a moment of misery without understanding the miracle potential!

REFLECT ON THIS

- How can you open your heart to allow God to meet you where you are?
- How have you misread situations before that caused you to miss your miracle?
- Who are the angels that God placed in your life to minister to you?
- Do you feel God is obligated to respond to all of your requests? Why or why Not?
- When was the last time you had to trust God?

CHAPTER 4

Beauty of Being Broken

"Whenever you're in conflict with someone, there is one factor that can make the difference between damaging your relationship and deepening it. The factor is attitude."

—William James

In 2003, after one year filled with a roller coaster ride of emotional highs and lows, the Bishop decided that my journey at Curry Temple had come to an end. I had an opportunity to say my goodbyes to the beautiful people of Curry Temple, and it was such a sad time that it left my heart to crumble into pieces. We all had felt something that we hadn't experienced before, and that was hope realized through the building of the Curry Temple. I was clear that it was not my purpose to stay at Curry Temple, so I packed my family and moved to the city of the Oakland.

I was appointed as pastor of the Beebe Memorial Cathedral, a historic church in Oakland, California. When I arrived, we had two worship services in a sanctuary that could comfortably seat fifteen hundred attendees. The first

Sunday I preached, attendance at the first service was only eight people, and there were seventy-three at the second service. The average age of members at Beebe Memorial Cathedral was over seventy years old. Despite some modest growth in my first year, we lost forty-seven members to death, and by the second year, an additional thirty-eight. I was losing more members to heaven than I was bringing into the Kingdom on earth! Additionally, when I arrived, the church carried more than $1 million in debt. It appeared that our demise was imminent.

The Lord had called me to serve a church that had, for the most part, lost its purpose and desire to be a thriving church. I was quickly discovering that, for so few members, there was a lot of conflict at Beebe Memorial Cathedral. What I knew was that God sent me to grow the church and, ultimately, to become the leader He desired me to be. My first year, though, most of my time was spent conducting funerals and refereeing fights in church business meetings! The assembly Methodists call "church conference" includes but is not limited to: paying bills, receiving reports from ministries, and making decisions regarding the direction of the church. It was in one church conference that, against my will, my role changed from being a referee of conflicts to being a boxer engaged in one!

I was presiding over the church conference as senior pastor, and it was my responsibility to set the agenda for the meeting and chair the meeting. Little did I know that there was a group within the small membership who wanted to derail the meeting. One agenda item I couldn't have dreamed would cause conflict became the unlikely thread that would unravel the fabric of the whole meeting: the Smokie Norful Gospel Concert.

We'd had great success with our first ever live gospel concert. We invited a major performing artist and filled the church to capacity. There was a member, who I'll call Ms. White, who wanted to challenge the report that the concert had been successful. She demanded to know where all the people had come from who filled the church. I couldn't tell her where they'd come from, but I shared with excitement that we promoted and marketed the show for people to come to our church and celebrate in praise.

We had a beautiful sanctuary, and invited visitors who didn't have a church home to consider Beebe Memorial as their place of worship. Also, we made a profit that evening to help with our insurmountable debt. To be quite honest, we needed the new members and new resources as ours were quickly drying up before our eyes. Knowing that those who worked with me to make this happen were enthused about what we had accomplished, I thought this great report would delight everyone at the meeting. Somehow Ms. White didn't like what she heard.

In fact, she became belligerent and threatened to sue me, announcing, "I don't have to take this, and I will see you at 1225 Fallon Street."

I didn't know the address, but later discovered it was the courthouse! Yes, at twenty-nine years old, I was sued for conducting a church conference.

Conflict is Unavoidable

Conflict is unavoidable. We are going to have conflict whether we like or not. It's a natural part of life.

However, just because we face conflict, it doesn't have to outdo us. The key is understanding why conflict occurs and a developing a strategy to walk through conflict so that relationships can be preserved.

Though conflict is stressful as we're dealing with it, we can turn it around for good. What matters most is how we handle the conflict.

Unfortunately, a lot of folks avoid conflict at all costs. If they've been hurt or jaded by their experiences of conflict, they may avoid it like the plague. Maybe that's you. Maybe you've faced conflict at home, at work, at church, or in your neighborhood, and it left you stinging. Perhaps you reason that if you just keep a safe distance from the person you're in conflict with, that things will get better with time.

The reality is that things will not get better. And sometimes they become worse! When you live like this, you compromise the abundant life you could be experiencing by settling for a mediocre imitation of the life you could be enjoying. Nothing grows without some level of conflict.

A Chinese proverb says, "A gem cannot be polished without friction, nor a man perfected without trials." Just like gemstones, people are refined through the process of facing and overcoming trials. This sharpening process helps you grow and transform into the person that God designed you to become. The conflict inherent in trials drives us to depend on God in every area of our lives. Conflict is an opportunity for the Lord to reveal His grace.

I recently saw a social media post that read, "God said 'love your enemy,' and I obeyed Him by loving myself." Inner conflict is an opportunity to look in the mirror and love the part of you that isn't on display. You cannot become a better version of yourself if you avoid the challenges, difficulties, and adversities in your life.

Moments of Conflict

Conflict comes in all shapes and sizes. Sometimes it's as major as a church member who files a lawsuit. But conflicts can also be as minor as a change in schedule that interferes with your plans. For example, the utility company assures you that they can be done with work in your home by noon, but they don't show up until noon. Each conflict, large or small, requires a different tool to handle the challenge effectively. Working through conflict also requires you to be your best self. If you're up for that challenge, get ready to grow.

Over the course of twenty-six years in ministry and twenty-one years in full-time pastoral ministry, I have handled a variety of conflicts, personally and professionally, that have stretched me beyond what I thought I could manage. One of the largest came about fourteen years ago, when I first became Senior Pastor of Beebe Memorial CME Cathedral. Generally speaking, the first year can often feel like pastoral honeymoon. It's time to spend time with folks and get to know them. Unfortunately, this wasn't my experience! My time there lasted only ninety days, until that fateful church meeting about the gospel concert.

Fallout

I didn't take Ms. White's threats seriously, at first, figuring it was just talk. But months later, when I opened the mail on a Monday afternoon following the Sunday of my pastoral appreciation, I realized I was wrong. In a large stack of mail was an envelope from the circuit court system addressed to yours truly. Ms. White had alleged that I threw her out of the church. Her accusation was odd, since ten other members present had seen her stomp out of her own accord.

However legitimate or illegitimate, I was devastated, scared, enraged, and embarrassed. What had I done to deserve this? Whether or not I liked it, this was my new reality. I wasn't looking forward to facing it, but I had to. I knew that how I handled this conflict would determine how the rest of the congregation viewed me.

I immediately sought counsel regarding the small claims suit. My attorney suggested that I file a counter suit so that the case could go to court and be represented by a lawyer who could defend my name. The counter suit would also allow me to continue to focus on pastoral ministry and my doctoral studies at the time. All of it made me wildly uncomfortable. I'd never been sued and I'd never sued anyone. In the quiet hours of the night, I started to wonder what the members, leaders, Bishop, and my family would think of me. I was forced to wrestle with my identity as a child of God, family man, and senior pastor as I fought for what was right. The conflict lasted more than a year, and included plenty of other drama-filled moments. I hoped that a scheduled arbitration session would make Ms. White's intentions, and those of a small group within the church, clear.

I stood outside the door of arbitration chamber for about forty-five minutes as my attorney and members of the small group conducted the meeting with Ms. White. The anticipation was stressful, as I had to trust someone else to decide my fate! Finally, everyone in the room walked out of the meeting. As she passed, Ms. White looked at me, but didn't say a word. I quickly headed toward my attorney and asked the results. He told me that when he informed the eighty-one-year-old that she faced potential perjury charges, she immediately told the truth. She confessed that she, and a small group from the church, didn't want me as their pastor because I was too young. The suit had been an attempt to get rid of me. They'd hoped that the pressure of the conflict would make me quit. My attorney told me that, in light of her confession, the arbitrator had banned Ms. White from the church, with the exception of attending funerals and weddings.

The moment he delivered the news, I felt hurt and rejected because I wasn't wanted as a pastor. Their opinion had nothing to do with my pastoral gifts or skills, but was all about my age. Nevertheless, a strange sense of peace came over me as I drove back to the church that day. I felt the affirmation of God over my life for the first time in several months. God had seen me through the conflict. It wasn't pretty, and there was no big crescendo at the end of the trial, but God had shepherded me through the dispute. Had I not recognized God's grace at that moment, I might have risked remaining bitter both at Ms. White and also at the rest of the members who'd supported her behavior. I felt broken by the ordeal, but also felt strangely blessed. (Though I quietly hoped she wouldn't choose to come to weddings or funerals!)

I prayed that God would keep me from becoming as hard-hearted as she'd become. A few months later, I had my first encounter with Ms. White since the arbitration. The chance meeting, at a local store, was as unpleasant as I'd worried it might be. But I kept my composure and didn't respond to her rants or her attacks upon my character. I spoke politely and continued with my day. Over the next months, Ms. White would visit the church for funerals. She would sit in the rear of the sanctuary and as soon as the service was over she would leave. This continued for about a year. Not only that, but on Sundays she would come into the narthex to peek in the window of the sanctuary door. But she'd never enter into worship and would leave before many noticed her being there.

One day, though, all of this behavior changed. One Sunday morning, as I prepared for worship, I felt in my spirit that Ms. White was going to show up to church that day. My intuition was correct. When I saw her frame darken the doors of the sanctuary, my stomach folded like fresh pretzel dough, waiting to be placed to bake in the oven. My emotions were all over the place, but I didn't know what to do or what to say. During the service, I sat in the pulpit anticipating my encounter with her. This time, I knew that meeting face to face would be unavoidable. She sat to my right side, and when I'd glance in her direction she'd look down or straight ahead. She never looked my way. That morning I stood, by God's grace, and preached his Word with everything I had in me.

I don't remember the title of the message that day, but I do remember walking down from the pulpit at the end of the service, inviting people to respond to the message by receiving the invitation to Christian discipleship. The invitation was the pivotal moment in service when people who are seekers of Christ, or those who desire a church home, can decide if this community is for them. Much to my surprise, many people came down the aisle to rededicate their lives to God.

In the middle of the small crowd of seekers stood Ms. White.

I was nervous and didn't know how to respond, so in my mind I braced myself for the worst. I quickly scrolled through questions I might ask about her purpose for being in worship and for walking down the aisle.

What did she want?

Why was she there?

Did she have a concealed weapon, and would she kill me?

Just kidding!

But I knew that she understood that she'd been banned from attending worship services. Yet she continued to walk down the aisle as others had done before her.

Ms. White walked up to me slowly, methodically, with a contrite look on her face. Knowing that she couldn't join the church, I leaned forward to hear her intentions.

She stated in a calm voice, "I want to give my life back to God."

I responded and said that God would always take her back into His heart. I welcomed her in that hour, not thinking that anything would change because she'd made the declaration of repentance, and continued to embrace others who were joining the church that day.

However, this wasn't the end of the story!

Ms. White actually became active in the church again, participating in Sunday school and senior ministry. She even started tithing! Only occasionally would she have outbursts of anger. Most of the members at that time, who'd known her, would agree that her behavior was heavenly compared to days' past.

After months of regular attendance, I stopped seeing Ms. White at church. I wondered where she might have been, but I was too guarded to reach out to learn why. A few months had passed when I received a phone call from a number that showed on my phone as being a nearby hospital. It was Ms. White! She was hospitalized and wanted me to visit her in the hospital immediately.

I contemplated not going, because I couldn't push from my mind all of the threatening messages, harassment, and embarrassment that I had endured from this woman. She'd made my life a living hell. Now she wanted me to visit her in the hospital? I couldn't imagine why she would want a pastoral visit from me after our history of conflict. My mind told me to steer clear, but my heart as prompting me to visit her. Eventually my heart won, and I went to the hospital to see her.

As I arrived, a security guard was standing outside of the door her room.

"This can't be good," I mused to myself.

As I approached the room, the security guard let me know that Ms. White was waiting for my arrival. I greeted her with a smile when I entered the room, and she asked me to come in and have a seat. Reluctantly, I sat down, but remained cautious since I didn't know the reason she'd requested a visit. I asked Ms. White why was there was a security guard standing at her room, and she shared that she'd just had a fight with the nurse and had thrown a bowl of soup at her. The security guard was there to ensure that she would remain civil to anyone who entered her room.

After I dragged a chair over beside her bed, Ms. White began, "I called you here because I wanted something from you."

"Okay," I replied cautiously, "What is it that you want?"

In a shaky and scratchy voice, she said six words I never imagined I'd hear this side of heaven, "I want you to forgive me!"

She began to share her heart as tears rolled down her face. Soon tears start to flow from my own eyes.

"In spite of all the things that I have done to you, you remained a perfect gentleman," she explained. "I didn't understand why, until now. God was showing me his grace through you. To be quite honest, I thought I wasn't deserving of his grace, not to mention his mercy. The day I walked down the aisle of the sanctuary sealed my conviction when you received me without judgment. It made me want to see you so I can ask you for forgiveness."

I couldn't believe what I was hearing.

Finally she begged, Pastor, please forgive me. I am sorry for what I've done to you."

Without thinking twice, I blurted out, "I forgive you!"

I was honest with Ms. White and told her it wasn't easy. I confessed that I'd felt compelled to run away—not from her, but from the situation. I couldn't explain why I didn't, but I did let her know that I knew I wasn't supposed to run away.

After this, our relationship drastically changed. It was remarkable to see, with my own eyes, how someone who had anger problems since the age of three—until she was eighty-four!—could experience the grace of God through conflict.

Lessons Learned

This battle, that I never would have chosen, began to teach me to search for God's grace even when it's not always easy always to recognize. It taught me to see grace in conflict. Now, I'm aware that this story could've ended in many other ways. But through this unlikely encounter I discovered that even destructive conflict, that frequently leads to resentment and anger, can lead to repentance and forgiveness when faced head on with courage and God's grace.

Proverbs 27:17, in Eugene Peterson's paraphrase of the Scriptures called *The Message*, exhorts, "You use steel to sharpen steel, and one friend sharpens another."

The Hebrew term translated here as "sharpen" means "to make or cause a person to be keen in perception, quick-witted, or full of energy." Another interpretation is, "As iron sharpens iron, close friends provide constructive criticism and accountability."[2] Just as sharpening an iron blade makes it more efficient, close friends sharpen one another's character.[3]

We're not sharpened when everything goes our way. Instead, our character is sharpened through conflict. Discussions, criticisms, suggestions, and ideas can all contribute to our growth. The grinding process—when life is more abrasive than we'd choose—need not destroy us. It can actually make us stronger. Some things in our lives, like useless chaff, may be eliminated through this process. And other things may come into clearer focus as a result of this sharpening. Some people you were hanging onto may be released from your life, if they were harmful to your growth and

2   Barry, J. D., Mangum, D., Brown, D. R., Heiser, M. S., Custis, M., Ritzema, E., ... Bomar, D. (2012, 2016). *Faithlife Study Bible* (Pr 27:17). Bellingham, WA: Lexham Press.

3   Barry, J. D., Mangum, D., Brown, D. R., Heiser, M. S., Custis, M., Ritzema, E., ... Bomar, D. (2012, 2016). *Faithlife Study Bible* (Pr 27:17). Bellingham, WA: Lexham Press.

development. I am convinced, though, that you will become stronger, sharper, and better-equipped if you offer the abrasive people and situations in your life to God, and submit to His guidance.

You may have thought that the conflicts you've faced were meant to cause you harm. But each one has shaped you into the person that you are right now. I suspect that some of the roughest seasons in your life have made you a better person. Perhaps you struggled to endure, but these challenges molded your character! When you persevered, you gained the tenacity that you needed to push through the mess and experience God's mercy. The situation that felt as though it would break you in two has changed your outlook on life. My encounter with Ms. White made me better and not bitter. And I know this can be your testimony as well.

Wisdom for the Journey

Do not allow your adverse circumstances to distract you from the reason you are in the situation in the first place. It's easy to get caught up in the minutiae and forget why it's so important to engage conflict head-on as we continue to live out the purposes God has for our lives. I had to remind myself over and over again that the reason that I had to endure was that God called me to serve and lead. Plain and simple! My calling was never meant be sidetracked because of trials.

No matter what conflict you face, God is bigger than your conflict. I wasn't designed to be a mediocre leader, and God was taking me to another level. When you face conflict, your purpose is to learn what you can in order to prepare yourself to advance to the next level of your journey. My purpose wasn't to win the battle, but to have faith that the fight was already won on my behalf. My goal was to fight so that I could gain the strength needed to continue to win. Being a winner won't always be smooth sailing. It's often hard work!

I love watching the Olympic Games because seeing the amazing victories and defeats inspires me. Athletes train for years in preparation for their competition, and sometimes they are disqualified. It is heartbreaking, but this is how you become better through conflict. While watching the 2016 Olympics, there was a race that I watched that I usually wouldn't have watched because I found it less exciting than the others. It wasn't the adrenaline-packed 100m sprint that I was watching, nor the 200m dash or relay race. Surprisingly, it was the longer 10,000m race that captured my attention. In the contest, the top runners from around the world were competing for the gold, and there was one runner who was favored to win: Britain's Mo Farah, a 33-year-old athlete. The games were held in Rio de Janeiro, where scores of people watched these accomplished athletes compete at the highest level. The intensity in the stadium could be seen on the runners' faces that were magnified on the screen.

The runners began the race and everyone looked strong for the first ten laps of the contest until something unusual happened. The formation of athletes began to shift as athletes moved to occupy the inside lanes. During the tenth lap of the twenty-five-lap race, Farah's training partner, Galen Rupp of the United States of America, tripped Mo Farah, who fell onto the track. He was trampled by a Kenyan runner, and many who were watching the race wondered if it was over for Farah. Staring at the screen in anticipation, I watched Mo Farah rise from the track after being tripped, kicked in the head, and trampled. With courage and determination, he began running again as the whole world watched.

Farah got up and quickly and signaled to his wife and friends with a thumbs-up sign that his race wasn't over. I interpreted the thumbs up to mean that he was okay, and he could keep running. Mo Farah kept running his race, found his stride, and began making up lost time. Despite his dramatic tumble during the race, Mo Farah managed to clinch his Olympic gold medal. Later in Rio he became the first man in forty years to win Olympic gold in two long-distance events when he won the 5,000m race. Falling face-first into the asphalt wasn't Farah's first stumble into conflict. Mo Farah would frequently be stopped by security officials in airports based on his Muslim name. One time he showed TSA Agents his gold medals, but they didn't matter because he was already a subject under suspicion. Farah has learned, over the years, to keep going in spite of life's tumbles.

There's a lot we can learn from Farah's story. Life will trip you, kick you in the head, and trample you, but if you are driven to finish the race, nothing can hold you back.

As Farah finished the 10,000m race, he kept glancing behind him. Though he continued to run the race with grace and consistent strides, the turning of his head seemed curious. At home on my couch, I silently wondered to myself why he kept looking back. Maybe, I guessed, he was looking back to remember the place where he'd fallen to mark how far he'd come while running his race.

Although a lot of us want to quickly move beyond that place where we failed, it's often worth revisiting, as a reminder that we have moved beyond where we once were.

You were made to win. Designed for victory, you were made to achieve greatness. The only way to get there, though, is to face life's hard knocks and agree with God that none are worthy to receive that victory. We are unworthy, but God uses unworthy people as His primary tool in redeeming the world.

Lessons for You

In the chapters ahead, I will offer some tools and practices that have helped me move beyond life's conflicts, allowing me to exchange brokenness for exceptional purpose.

God taught me the most about the beauty of being broken through conflicts I never would have chosen:

- Those who attack in a battle moment may not be attacking you personally, but what you represent.

- Have someone in your life who can help you see objectively in the midst of the chaos that you may be experiencing.
- Spend time with individuals who have been through conflict to discover what they've learned from their hard knocks.
- Listen to your heart.
- Ask God for the revelation of what you should see in the conflict.
- Always be aware of your capacity to handle conflict.

RECOGNIZE THIS

Conflict will happen. You can embrace it or run from it.

DO THIS

Commit to face conflict rather than run from it.

REFLECT ON THIS

- What have been some of the most challenging conflicts that you have experienced in your career, relationships, church, and family? How did you handle them?
- Consider this statement: "Conflict is the way that you develop into a healthy person."
  Do you agree or disagree? Explain your answer.
- Can you think of a time when you were involved in a conflict that went south? Did you ever recover from it? How?
- What was the unspoken message you inferred from the situation? (e.g. They don't respect me. They don't like me.)
- Why are you reading this book? What do you hope to get out of this book?

CHAPTER 5

Love Changes Things

Yolanda, single and in her early forties, strove to live a life of excellence. She was loved by her family and revered by her colleagues in the school where she worked as a teacher. She had a bubbly personality and was the life of the party. In one year, though, Yolanda's life changed. Like many, she began to experiences losses in her life as she matured. She lost both her mother and father to cancer within six months of each other, and then her fiancé broke off their relationship with little explanation. It was too much loss. Yolanda treasured her relationships and, within the course of a single year, her most valuable ones had ended.

In their absence, Yolanda was left with a terrible void in her life. Instead of dealing with her grief, though, Yolanda became increasingly mean to the people who would try to care for her. She stopped meeting with the girlfriends she used to have brunch with each Sunday. Most of them reached out to her, but she never returned their calls. At work, people noticed a change in Yolanda also. She was functional as a teacher, but the children were not excited to be in her class the way they'd once been because of the change in her mood and attitude.

One day Yolanda's best friend, Monica, decided enough was enough. She was determined to scale the wall Yolanda had erected around her life. Monica went to Yolanda's house on a Saturday, used her key to get in, and forced Yolanda to get out of bed and go to lunch. Predictably, Yolanda resisted. But, because of Monica's insistence, she finally begrudgingly went with her.

Sitting across from each other at an outdoor café, Yolanda was silent for the first twenty minutes. Monica was making small talk, and Yolanda just stared at her with a blank look. When the waitress came to take their order, Monica ordered her food, but Yolanda continued to sit there without saying a word to the server.

Confused, the server raised her eyebrows and let Monica know that she was going to put her order in to the kitchen.

Looking into Yolanda's vacant eyes, Monica said, "Hey friend, I didn't do anything for you to treat me like this and not return my phone calls. The least you can do is talk to me." Then, in case Yolanda had forgotten, she added, "I'm your best friend."

Averting her gaze from Monica, Yolanda looked down at her phone, fiddling with an app.

After several minutes of awkward silence, Monica complained, "Yolanda, I don't believe you. After all we have been through together, you won't talk to me?"

Yolanda stared at her, got up from the table, and left the restaurant. When a red Honda pulled up, Monica watched Yolanda slide into an Uber and leave without saying goodbye.

Though Monica was stinging inside from her friend's rude disrespect, she refused to give up on her friend.

Hurt People Hurt People

Does Yolanda's behavior feel familiar to you?

If it does, you may be all too familiar with the reality Monica encountered:

Hurt people hurt people. Whether they've been able to name it or not, far too many people have experienced hurt at the hands of someone who's hurting. Those who have experienced spiritual, physical, and emotional hurt from others have a tendency to inflict pain on those around them. I've certainly experienced this as a pastor, as I did with Ms. White. Not only have I endured this as a leader, but also as a nephew, brother, son, husband, father, and friend. Whether they're aware of it or not, people want you to feel the pain they've felt.

In my early twenties, some of my family members distanced themselves from me because they didn't like my father. I'd traveled to the city where they lived to visit them, but if I didn't go where they lived, they weren't even willing to make an effort to see me. I reached out to visit them whenever I'd be in town, but they never attempted to reciprocate. I didn't understand their odd behavior. In fact, the distance they tried to keep between us felt particularly hurtful because they were my own flesh and blood. I understood that the barrier stemmed back to conflicts my father had with them. But, in my mind, those didn't have anything to do with me.

Occasionally I would get a chance to see them, but those visits often left me feeling worse than when they ignored me!

Each time I'd convince myself, "They'll see how fun it could be to fellowship with family."

Yet, instead of this being a happy time for us to get to know each other, the opposite proved true. The longer I stayed, the more negative the experience became. I was not only hurt, but it made me stop trying.

I'd wondered, as a child, why they never visited us in Chicago. And when we would visit them in the South, it was always awkward. Though I didn't understand the root of this hurt when I was a boy, I eventually figured out why this particular rejection stung so much: no one ever wants to experience rejection and denial from the very ones that you call your own.

Me, Too

I've been a victim of hurt, and I'll admit that I've also been a perpetrator of pain. I've had moments in which I was the one who was hurting others because I was hurt.

Over the course of my life, I developed a coping mechanism to protect myself from getting hurt: I detached myself, emotionally and physically, from relationships that I felt were harmful to me. I did this, initially, because I didn't want to feel the void and heartache I experienced when I experienced pain. I began using this defense in childhood when I watched my mother struggle with her personal demons that left us in some bad situations. As a young child, I couldn't stand to see her hurting and I felt I felt a sense of responsibility to take care of her when she couldn't do so herself. As a boy, I felt stuck.

As a result, I learned to deny my emotions. I like to describe that coping strategy as my internal force field. It prevented me from getting hurt by people. This force field approach to pain and conflict worked for me as a child, but it became a weapon of mass destruction as an adult. If I suspected someone was going to hurt me or betray me, I would cut them off. If someone was in disagreement with me, I would stop talking to them and abruptly end the relationship. Once I learned how effective this strategy was to avoid pain, it became my weapon of choice. If someone offended me, I would cut them off. If I suspected I couldn't trust a person, I would cut them off and put up my force field. I'm not proud of this stage of my life. Now I can see that I was the hurt one who was hurting others. I'd cut them off to avoid dealing with the conflict that accompanied betrayal, frustration and mistrust.

Eventually, I had to face the reality that the behaviors that had protected me as a boy were no longer useful as an adult. With the help of a licensed counselor, I confronted the conflict of pain so I could trade my brokenness for exemplary purpose. And as I became healthier, I began to notice that I wasn't the only one. In fact, I began to recognize this pattern of behavior all around me.

Hurt people hurting people is like a leaky faucet that is hard to turn off once the drip has started. Most hurt people listen and see life through the filter of their own brokenness. The words and actions of others are interpreted through the lens of their own shattered thought processes. Hurt people often carry a spirit of victimization and frequently blame others for their predicament.

I began to notice hurt people who would explode with emotions far more intense than seemed appropriate for a given situation. These big feelings had more to do with the years of pain they'd endured, and never addressed, than what was actually happening in the moment. Yet individuals would become so self-absorbed with their pain that they'd be unaware that they were hurting others.

Yet I am living proof that change is possible. If you are willing, you can exchange your problems for a healthier life. The first step to fixing your problems is facing your pain.

Conflict in the Bible

As I survey the biblical landscape, I can see that hurt people hurting people is not a new phenomenon! The Hebrew Scriptures are filled with men and women who were hurt people who hurt people. When he shares his vision to build a wall for Jerusalem, Nehemiah records his encounter with some men who were hurting.

"Now when Sanballat heard that we were building the wall, he was angry and greatly enraged, and he jeered at the Jews. And he said in the presence of his brothers and of the army of Samaria, 'What are these feeble Jews doing? Will they restore it for themselves? Will they sacrifice? Will they finish up in a day? Will they revive the stones out of the heaps of rubbish, and burned ones at that?' Tobiah the Ammonite was beside him, and he said, 'Yes, what they are building—if a fox goes up on it he will break down their stone wall!' Hear, O our God, for we are despised. Turn back their taunt on their own heads and give them up to be plundered in a land where they are captives." (Neh. 4:1-4 ESV)

The writer describes his assailant as angry, enraged, and jeering. These words suggest that Sanballat, intent on ridiculing the work of God, had some hurt inside. Warren Wiersbe explains, "British critic and author Thomas Carlyle called ridicule 'the language of the devil.'" He adds, "Some people who can stand bravely when they are shot at will collapse when they are laughed at. Shakespeare called ridicule 'paper bullets of the brain,' but those bullets have slain many a warrior."[4]

Sanballat and his friends had begun to ridicule the Jews before the work on the wall had even started! He called them feeble which means "withered or miserable." In his view, the Jews were like cut flowers who were withering and fading away. He ridiculed their work by asking three insulting questions. He questioned their ability, capacity, and strength. Sanballat and Tobiah were experts on the problems of others but had no intention of offering them solutions. It was deflating to the people of Israel and potentially damaging to Nehemiah. This kind of hurt can cause dangerous repercussions.

The things people say can sometimes hurt us. As I was growing up, people used to say, "Sticks and stones may break my bones, but words will never hurt me." This may be true for some, but for most of us this is false. The poison of ridicule is so intense it can disrupt our thinking and disfigure our self-esteem. Contempt leads to discouragement, and discouragement is one of the enemy's favorite tools to defeat us. Hurt people can be used by the enemy to keep us from reaching our potential and living out God's calling purposes for our lives.

---

4   Wiersbe, W. W. (1996). Be Determined (pp. 50–51). Wheaton, IL: Victor Books.

There Are Answers to the Hurt

Nehemiah offered a solution that strengthened them in their struggle. He prayed to God and asked for help.

To avoid being wounded by those who are wounded, hurt by those who are hurting, your immediate response to their fiery assaults should be prayer. Prayer worked for Nehemiah, and it works for me. Finding freedom through prayer trumps nursing hurts any day of the week. In the fourth verse of the fourth chapter of Nehemiah, we see Nehemiah praying unto God in an unusual way. He prayed and asked God to fight his enemies for him. He didn't use his energy to reply to their negative words, but he focused his energy on the power of God. That gave him divine results.

Prayer keeps us from perseverating on words of ridicule and on people who do not have any power over us. Prayer keeps us from giving significant time to insignificant people. Prayer is the catalyst that keeps your focus on the work God has for you. Prayer concentrates our minds on the weapons God gave us to use when we face a spiritual battle that is born from hurt. In spite of the brokenness you've endured, your enemies can't stop the success that you will experience when you offer that brokenness to God.

In fact, Jesus the Christ had to deal with hurt people, just as we do. Jesus modeled how to handle the kind of injured people who can hurt you if you allow it. He remained calm, and didn't react as someone who'd lost control. He demonstrated power by choosing to remain under control. He did this silently in some hostile situations. In others, when He gained an audience with His haters, He asked questions and pointed his listeners to the Word of God. We see this most clearly in a story John recounts in the eighth chapter of his gospel,

> "'Abraham is our father,' they answered.
>
> 'If you were Abraham's children,' said Jesus, 'then you would do what Abraham did. As it is, you are looking for a way to kill me, a man who has

told you the truth that I heard from God. Abraham did not do such things. You are doing the works of your own father.'" (John 8:39–41a)

In case you didn't catch it, He just insinuated that they were more likely children of the devil than children of Abraham.

> "'We are not illegitimate children,' they protested. 'The only Father we have is God himself.'
>
> Jesus said to them, 'If God were your Father, you would love me, for I have come here from God. I have not come on my own; God sent me. Why is my language not clear to you? Because you are unable to hear what I say. You belong to your father, the devil, and you want to carry out your father's desires. He was a murderer from the beginning, not holding to the truth, for there is no truth in him. When he lies, he speaks his native language, for he is a liar and the father of lies. Yet because I tell the truth, you do not believe me! Can any of you prove me guilty of sin? If I am telling the truth, why don't you believe me? Whoever belongs to God hears what God says. The reason you do not hear is that you do not belong to God.'" (John 8:41b–47)

This was an ancient "who's your daddy" moment. And, hurt, they turn it right back around onto Jesus,

> "The Jews answered him, 'Aren't we right in saying that you are a Samaritan and demon-possessed?'
>
> 'I am not possessed by a demon,' said Jesus, 'but I honor my Father and you dishonor me. I am not seeking glory for myself; but there is one who seeks it, and he is the judge. Very truly I tell you, whoever obeys my word will never see death.'
>
> At this they exclaimed, 'Now we know that you are demon-possessed! Abraham died and so did the prophets, yet you say that whoever obeys your word will never taste death.'" (John 8:48–51)

In this exchange, Jesus models how to handle hurt when you come in contact with those who are determined to wound you with their rhetoric and bad intentions. Jesus shows us that it is possible to diffuse hurt with healthy behavior. Fighting back with hurtful words is simply using the tool of the enemy. No one wins when force is used on any level. Rather, there is a more excellent way. Jesus demonstrates this more excellent way in his Sermon on the Mount,

> "But to you who are listening I say: Love your enemies, do good to those who hate you, bless those who curse you, pray for those who mistreat you. If someone slaps you on one cheek, turn to them the other also. If someone takes your coat, do not withhold your shirt from them. Give to everyone who asks you, and if anyone takes what belongs to you, do not demand it back. Do to others as you would have them do to you. "If you love those who love you, what credit is that to you? Even sinners love those who love them" (Luke 6:27-32).

The way to respond to hurt is with love! Love is an unconditional commitment to people who are imperfect. This kind of love is demonstrated to us by Jesus Christ on a cross that He didn't deserve. He gave His life for those who hurt him. He not only preached love, but He practiced love in the sacrifice of His own life. This is love. Maybe you're not willing to give up your life for those who mistreat you and hurt you. I understand that hesitation. But you can make a choice to love. You are called to love deeply until the hurt you've endured is traded for wholeness. Peter writes, "Above all, love each other deeply, because love covers over a multitude of sins" (1 Pet. 4:8).

Spread Love

One of the greatest joys that I experience, on a frequent basis as the leader of our faith community, is the miracle of love transforming people. I have the privilege to hear the testimony of those who share with me how God's love touched their hearts and changed something in their lives.

In one instance, it was a brother who shared with me as I picked up a sandwich from the local bagel shop. He offered generous expressions of gratitude about how the church had blessed him and his girlfriend. He shared with me how they had been struggling with whether or not to give up their son. They were struggling financially and faced other challenges that made caring for him difficult. They walked into the church, and on that particular Sunday the emphasis of the service was centered on children and babies. They were shocked that, out of all the Sundays they could have decided to come to church, this would be the one. He went on to tell me that it was the love they saw and felt in the church that Sunday that helped them change their minds about keeping their son. Today they are a family and are expecting a baby girl.

There is another story that was shared with me from a member within our community. Janice, in her mid-fifties, said that before she joined our church she hadn't seen or spoken to her son in over ten years. As they stood together at the altar one Sunday Morning, she shared with tears in her eyes that for ten years she'd had no contact with him or his young family. On this particular Sunday, her son James agreed to see her again if they came to church. I learned that the two had been estranged based, in part, on what he was told about his mother early in his childhood when she wasn't involved in raising him. James was raised by his father and was told that his mother didn't want anything to do with him.

I could only imagine the depth of rejection that this young man felt after being told that the woman who birthed him didn't want any part of his life. My heart hurt for them as I considered being separated from my children for even a month. I couldn't imagine what it would be like not to see them for years.

Graciously, I was able to hear the rest of the story. Janice had struggled with addictions, and the goal of James' father was to protect his son at all costs. The father didn't want any part of the life that Janice was living, so, out of the hurt that happened within their broken relationship, he'd planted this seed of rejection within James. For most of his childhood, this seed of distrust germinated and became a stronghold in James's life. He believed that his mother didn't want him.

James had only seen his mother in pictures. And the moment he was old enough to be on his own, Janice showed up in his life. But then for ten years she hadn't see him again, until that day in the church.

Curious, I queried, "How did this happen? How were you able to come back together?"

With tears in her eyes, Janice responded, "I never gave up on loving my son." Then, she added, "There was not one day that passed when I lost hope in the love I had for my child. My love for him helped me battle my demons and win. But I knew that being sober wasn't enough."

She paused to wipe the tears from her cheeks.

She continued, "I needed a place that represented love so that we could open up the dialogue again. I called him, and I knew Mother's weekend was coming and asked him to come to church with me. He agreed."

A huge smile broke out across Janice's face.

"I know that he loves me," she added, "because he showed up to see me, and now we are going to have dinner and begin a long overdue conversation."

Janice and James were loved back to life, and the church became the place where they experienced love again.

No More Tears

One of the most riveting encounters that I've ever experienced was visiting the men who live in California's San Quentin Prison. This prison is known to house some of the most notorious and violent offenders who ever walked the streets of the United States of America. Many of them *earned* the reputation, but others were housed in that prison who were wrongly convicted and simply not given a chance.

As I talked to some of the "lifers," those serving a life sentence without the possibility of parole, I heard an interesting story. They shared how they are making a difference in the community through their No More Tears program. No More Tears is a non-profit, operated within the walls of San Quentin Prison, with the goal of helping prepare inmates for life outside prison, so they don't ever have to return. I was shocked how politically engaged this group of men was, and how they had a genuine concern for people and living the best lives they could.

As we toured the facility, which felt like it was stuck in the industrial age, we paused to sit in a cold room to listen to one inmate share his story of transformation. The man's name was Lee. I'm not sure if it was his real name, but it's what everybody called him. Convicted of murder, Lee was in prison for life. But eventually Lee had reached a point when he knew he needed to meet the family of the man's life he'd taken and try to make things right. So mediators arranged for him to meet the family. When they met, he expressed to them how much he regretted taking the life of their loved one and asked for forgiveness from the family.

However, some of the family members who came began to scream at him and say ugly words. Lee shared that it took every bit of strength to bear their anger. But he received it, because he felt he deserved it. However, he told us with remorse, something slowly began to change in the room.

Lee explained, "His mother wanted to speak to me, and I was scared of what she would say. She said, with tears rolling down her face, 'I forgive you.' And then she got up from her seat and start walking toward me."

He paused to gather his composure before continuing.

"As the guards stood alert," he explained, "she hugged me."

I waited to hear what happened next.

Lee explained, "That was my transformation. She gave me something that I didn't deserve: *love*. I met with them to change things for them, and it ended up changing me. Through that mother, I experienced love in a whole new way. I will never forget that talk we had that gave me a new outlook on life in prison, where loving your enemy has a full meaning."

Love changed Lee.

Adversity Activates Your Love!

When your enemy maligns you, you alone choose your attitude. That's what the mother of the man Lee had killed did. Like her, you can choose to exchange hurt for love.

If you want to live life with exemplary purpose, you must be prepared to handle the disparagement that comes your way. Ideally, you will reach a point when you're able to release the expectations you have of others. As you release expectations of others, you release the expectation that the love you offer will be reciprocated. When you release the expectation that your efforts will be appreciated, your genius will be discovered, or your love will be received, you are set free. Love others anyway!

This isn't work you can do alone. You don't have to muster the energy and courage to love from your own resources. Rather, the new capacity to love is a work of grace by God's Holy Spirit. God's power is at work in your heart, equipping you to love those who have hurt you. Don't worry, though, God is not asking you to become a glutton for punishment! Neither am I. But the more that you are willing to open yourself to the work of God's Spirit, the greater capacity you will have to love your enemy. When you are willing to embrace vulnerability, God's power is at work in you to love the way He loves.

God teaches you to release what leaves you incapacitated. When you release your own hurt, God supplies the fuel that gives you more capacity to love. This release happens when you exchange the pain you are holding for forgiveness. Is there someone in your life from whom you've withheld forgiveness? If you have not done so, it's time for you to forgive! Forgiveness is never about the person that hurt you. It is always about you releasing the power they had over you! When you forgive, you say to your enemy, "You cannot control me."

Extend Grace

When your enemy rejects you or judges you, it isn't actually about you. It's more about their own hurt, lack, limitations, and insecurities. I know that it still stings. But remember, it's not about you. Your worth and value aren't predicated upon the validation of other people because you were affirmed and loved before the foundations of the earth. God did that! And since God did this, you can extend the same grace that He's given to you to your enemies. That's right! Offer your enemy grace. Though the enemy will try to convince you that forgiveness makes you vulnerable to being hurt again, it's actually an opportunity for you to grow and move forward.

The wisdom literature of the Old Testament explains,

"If your enemy is hungry, give him food to eat;
if he is thirsty, give him water to drink.
In doing this, you will heap burning coals on his head,
and the LORD will reward you." (Prov. 25:21-22)

God rewards those who extend grace to their enemies. The rewards include peace of mind, security, and, most of all, love. Don't be surprised if your enemy experiences a degree of uneasiness because of your generosity. They may be wondering, "Why is this person so nice to me after all I have done to them?" In time they will discover that you are offering love because God has done the same for you. In spite of all of your flaws, imperfections, shortcomings, and failings, God still loves you and accepts you as a permanent child in his Kingdom. For this reason you can continue to extend grace to your enemies by looking beyond their faults and recognizing their needs.

Everybody wants to be loved and happy, but nobody wants to put in the work that makes love real. Some people become depressed by dwelling on the love that's missing from their lives. But God never intended our misery! Nothing will make you feel loved until you choose to receive the love God has for you. You have to make the exchange!

The Meaning of Exchange

To exchange is to give one thing and receive another—especially of the same type or value—in return. If your life was like a checking account, people would be able to interpret the meaning of your story by what you spend and withdraw, or "exchange." None of us desires to have a checking account that is overdrawn and piled up with overdraft fees, costing more in the long run. We all wish for our accounts to show a healthy balance.

When you have a balance in your account, it will eventually lead to more benefits and rewards. The higher your balance, the greater your value to the banking relationship. This principle works in all of your relationships; not just in the banking industry! If you allow people to make more withdrawals than deposits in your life, by mistreating or abusing you, you are out of balance and in the negative. Know when to close the account. Know when to step away from a relationship that's death-dealing.

No balance, no value!

Know your balance and then you will know your value.

Worth the Work

When you're in relationship with people who are hurting, there's a lot you can't control. You can't control what they think, what they say, or what they do. The only thing you can control is how you respond to them. If you react to their brokenness, you'll struggle to live out your exceptional purpose. Until you're willing to exchange your own brokenness for the grace God offers you, you'll continue to get tangled up in the hurts of others.

Remember Monica and Yolanda? Monica chose not to respond in hurt after being hurt by her friend. In fact, she continued to get together with Yolanda each weekend, restoring their friendship and nurturing Yolanda's broken heart. Love won! With the loving support of her best friend, Yolanda was able to finally grieve her losses.

If you're willing to humble yourself, and love the way Jesus loved sinners like you, you can live in God's power that flows through your earthen vessel as you move into living out your exceptional purpose.

Lessons for You

- Love your way into your enemy's heart and watch God for the transformation!
- Forgiveness is the lever you pull to exchange the brokenness for your purpose.
- You have to confront your hurt to experience healing!

RECOGNIZE THIS

Whatever they say about you, always remember who you are: A person who matters to God.

DO THIS

Send a random expression of kindness (i.e. a post card, a handwritten note, an email, or text) to someone who hurt you and say, "I love you and you matter to me!"

REFLECT ON THIS

- What relationship that has been broken in your life you can mend?
- Do you have real enemies or perceived enemies? Why?
- Have you ever been really hurt in your life? How did you handle the pain that you experienced?
- Who are the people that you hurt? Did you feel the need, at any point, to reconcile?
- How hard do you love?

CHAPTER 6

The Potter Wants to Put You Back Together Again

This past year Chicago had the highest number of gun-related deaths of any city in America. Over 3,500 shootings resulted in over 750 murders. Most of those shootings have been localized in neighborhoods like the one in which I grew up.

My experience growing up in Chicago wasn't as desperate as the situation facing young people today. Yes, we had gangs that were a part of the cultural DNA. And certain streets weren't safe to travel at night. Or, sometimes, during the day. Race and social class segregated neighborhoods, as they do today, and most people I knew struggled to make ends meet. In the midst of all the craziness of our windy city, though, there were pockets of hope and possibility. One place of hope for my friends and me was Tuley Park. Tuley Park was located in the Chesterfield community.

Tuley Park had more than twenty acres of lush green grasslands with a gymnasium, auditorium, and multipurpose clubrooms. The exterior of the park featured lighted tennis courts, baseball diamonds, a large pool, a gazebo, and so much more. Every day after school we'd walk from my elementary school, at 650 East 91st Place, one block to 501 East 91st Place. Tuley Park was our home away from home. It was a place that kept most of us out of trouble. Growing up in the eighties, most of the kids in my neighborhood were latchkey kids. Latchkey kids were children who wore a key around their necks, or had a key safety pinned inside their clothing, to get into our homes afterschool, since most of our parents were working.

A bunch of my friends would leave Burnside Scholastic Academy every day and walk the city block to Tuley Park. We didn't want to sit at home alone, so we went to the park just to stay busy. We played all of the sports that were available at the park, including baseball, (which I wasn't good at) basketball, and tumbling. When our sports weren't in season, we would sign up for the other afterschool offerings. The class I was most excited about was drama. Honestly, I imagined myself becoming the next Denzel Washington. We were reading the 1949 play written by Arthur Miller, "Death of a Salesman," and it didn't seem to me like any of the roles Denzel Washington was playing. So imagine my surprise when my drama teacher encouraged me to sign up for the pottery class instead! Apparently, I was no Denzel. From the outside, it didn't make sense. Why would a little boy from the south side of Chicago join a pottery class? I was not feeling this class until I ran into my friend, John, who told me that the finest girls in the neighborhood were in the class. I immediately ran up to my teacher, and asked, "Hey, where do I sign up?"

Potter in Training

I wanted the girls to see my sensitive side. Just kidding. (Well, maybe a little.) When I walked into the room where the girls were already doing pottery, there was pottery everywhere. I saw smooth unglazed bowls, lumpy mugs, spindly vases, and other imaginative clay creations.

Each week, Pam, our instructor, invited us to join her for an enchanting journey into the world of pottery. The dusty room filled with unspeakable treasures fascinated me. I'd often sneak in before class just to gaze at the tables and shelves lined with ceramic creations. Sun peeked through the blinds of the room, highlighting a display of brilliant colors the glimmered from the finished pieces of pottery. Some of the pieces looked very expensive. One vase stood about four feet tall, and was wrapped in a dark candy apple red color. A rich cream trim lent it the elegance of a masterpiece. I was drawn toward this particular vase because I had never seen anything like it before. Pam had given us clear instructions to look and not touch the pottery. The craftspeople, she explained, had put countless hours into creating these beautiful vessels.

Awestruck, I asked, "Can I make something as beautiful as this one day?"

"If you want to put in the time and energy to be a potter," Pam answered, "you can learn how."

In that wonderful moment I forgot about the girls in the class and became enamored, instead, with the possibilities of the masterpieces I'd be able to create with my own hands.

Pam was a kind teacher who poured her heart into her eager students. We began by learning to glaze pre-formed ceramic pieces. We'd read the labels of colors that didn't yet look like the "turquoise" or "emerald" that their packaging promised. Pam taught us how to paint these glazes onto the pieces, and when we went home we'd leave them for her to fire in the kiln. It felt almost magical that we could leave our creations with Pam on a Friday, and when we returned on Monday it was as if they'd come to life! I made my mother a delicate ceramic rose and finished several other pieces as well, such as Mickey and Donald Duck. The pre-made molds gave us the opportunity to vivify a variety of projects. I enjoyed the work we were doing, but my eyes were set on something more advanced.

I wanted to learn how to operate the potter's wheel.

Every day that I walked through the doors of the workshop, my eyes drifted to the area where the adult potters were creating their masterpieces. Seeing them squeezing the wet clay, and carefully shaping it with the curve of their hands or the pressure of a single finger quickened my imagination. Something within me wanted to belong this group of creatives. Every day I'd ask Pam when it would be my turn to move on to the next level.

"When can I learn how to do the wheel?" I'd beg.

Calmly, she'd always answer, "When you are ready."

Her words still speak volumes to me today. She taught me that it's not wise to rush into a situation, task, or responsibility without proper preparation.

We were coming to the end of our class for the quarter, and I continued to beg Pam for the opportunity to try to become a potter. Finally, my persistence paid off, and Pam agreed. I was excited to finally be entering the big leagues of pottery.

As the other kids painted their projects, Pam sat me down beside her at the potter's wheel. I'd watched the other potters and felt like I was going to be a natural. Pam placed a lump of clay on my wheel and, as her foot gently pressed the floor pedal, she began to instruct me how to use my hands to shape the clay into a form. This was my big moment! I was a little nervous because I knew I didn't want to go back to painting pre-formed artwork. I didn't want to mess up this opportunity.

"Charley," Pam coached, "I need for you to take the lump of clay and center it on the wheel. It is important that every part of your lump of clay lines up with the center of the wheel."

Though I did exactly as she'd instructed me to do, it still felt like the venture went wrong from the beginning. For starters, the clay was unruly. It began to wobble all over the wheel, spilling out in all directions. I couldn't control the material and the process frustrated me to no end.

Being Shaped

The unwieldiness of that clay isn't so different from what it's like to follow God's will for our lives.

I'll be the first to admit that when I wanted my life to go in a certain way, I was often unruly.

For several years at Beebe Memorial Cathedral, I worked continually, without rest or a real vacation. I became an insane workaholic, getting high off of whatever the next achievement would be. Deluded, I began to believe that the work of the church couldn't continue without me. To be fair, my grandiosity was confirmed when I'd miss a Sunday, to speak someplace else, and attendance in worship would decline dramatically! My pattern wasn't healthy and I became burned out. Even my health began to fail. My stress was at an all-time high. I continued to function, but my creativity and passion were compromised.

Unwilling to be tamed, I'd headed off in a variety of different directions. Nothing in my life was making sense, and it was a season of unproductivity. God's hands were trying to center to me on the wheel of my purpose, but I wanted my way and I ended up being a hot mess. I was busy moving in life, but nothing was taking form. I suspect God's hand was present to guide me, but I wasn't pliable to His will and His purposes.

As Pam continued to teach me how to mold the clay, my forehead started to sweat profusely because I didn't know what to do to control it. The clay seemed as if it had a mind of its own. I thought it was me—that I was a particularly poor potter—but I quickly discovered that I was only struggling because I was a beginner. Learning to control the clay was all part of the process.

In a calm voice, Pam coached, "Stay focused, Charley."

I felt like there was some magic secret I was missing.

"Add some water to the clay," she offered.

I knew that adding water to the clay would make it more pliable. Dipping my hand in the bowl of water beside the wheel, I brought my hands back up to dampen the disobedient lump in front of me.

"Now press your hands evenly against the side of the clay," she coached, "and push it closer to the wheel head."

The wheel head was at the center of the wheel.

"Now take your hand," she instructed, "and smooth all of the uneven places and press in the rough areas."

Easier said than done, I thought to myself.

In one sense, this appears to be how God moves within our lives. God allows the Holy Spirit to soften us, making us more amenable to accepting

God's purpose for our lives. The hand of God fashions you to into the vessel He desires. The process, of course, requires that you allow the Lord to smooth out the unevenness in you and to massage out every rough place. Once you agree to be formed by the Spirit, God's hands start to guide you as you seek His purpose.

Even though I followed Pam's instruction to the letter, I still only created a wetter, messier lump of clay! I was devastated and disappointed because I felt as though I'd blown my chance. Succeeding with the pottery wasn't just about succeeding by following Pam instructions, it was also about gaining her acceptance.

One of the challenges I faced growing up was that I wanted very much to please my father. We developed a great relationship in my adult years, before he passed, but as a child I was riddled with issues around acceptance and rejection because I wanted his approval. As I moved into adulthood, I discovered that I wasn't the only one who struggled to please the one person whose love I most desired.

In a relationship like this, it doesn't matter what you attain, achieve, or accomplish. No matter what you do, you can never please the person or gain their approval. And this yearning to be accepted can leave you looking for love in all the wrong places, and craving attention from all the wrong people.

As I sat in front of a misshapen ball of clay, I thought it was over for me when I didn't get it right the first time. I assumed that Pam would reject me and I'd never get to become the potter I dreamed I could be.

Little did I know, the process wasn't over. It was just beginning.

With great compassion, Pam looked at me and said, "You can't give up now. You must start over." Then she added, "Trust the process and have more patience with the clay!"

I followed her instructions and, the second time, my lump of clay began to take form.

I discovered that I might not yet know the main key to success, but I did recognize that impatience was a guaranteed fail. I learned it is important to have patience with one's self in order to develop into the person God intended.

As I spent more time behind the wheel, my fingers started to feel like guides for the clay, instructing it what to do and when to do it. My eyes lit up with excitement as I began to see a creation forming out of nothing. The brownish-gray clay became one with my hands. They were there to guide the clay to becoming a masterpiece. As I began to relax, the lump in front of me began to take shape. At the end of the day I was enthused and anxious to try again.

The Next Day and the Next Level

The following day, I couldn't wait to finish school and run back to Tuley Park. I wanted to see if what I learned the day before would work again on the clay. After chatting with my friends John and Chris, I put my belongings away, put on my dark blue canvas apron, and headed to the pottery room. The previous day I'd learned how to get the clay to change form, but it wasn't a full vessel yet. Today was the day I believed that I was moving on to the next stage of the process. I sat back down with Pam and was able to begin working with the clay that I had used the previous day. I had created a form in the shape of a volcano, but the problem was there was no opening.

I needed an opening that could turn my volcanic shaped cone into a bowl, cup, or a vase, like I'd seen when I started the class. Pam coached me to start spinning the wheel, and I rested my left hand on the outside of the clay. Using my right hand, I pressed into the top of the clay. I carefully scooped out the excess clay and put it aside. As I opened up an empty space in the clay, I began to see my work starting to take shape.

In our spiritual lives, we have to surrender to the guidance of God's hands. Our part is to be open to allow God to press in. This acceptance is akin to "receiving" brokenness. When we allow ourselves to be pressed, broken, molded, we can become better available to hold something that we are destined to carry.

As a result of this process, I've been able to pay close attention to the ways of *the* Potter. But it wasn't just the Potter's hands—I also learned about the Potter's feet! The earthly potter has a little treadle as his foot, which he uses to control the speed of the wheel. This is critical because if it goes too fast, it could interfere with the process of the formation. So, the potter selects the right speed and tempo to make sure that the clay is not ruined in the process of creation.

The Potter not only guides the direction of your progress, but He also determines how fast you will get there. Some people find this disturbing, but for others it is comforting to know that the Potter won't rush you into something that you are not prepared to handle.

I remember hearing Peter Scazzero say, "When you are always traveling at warp speed you will end up with a warped life." I don't know about you, but I don't desire to live a life that has been warped because I started spinning out of control without God's feet controlling the speed. The right speed suggests that you are living a balanced life. With proper balance you can become the person that God designed you to be.

Formed for His Glory

One theological concept I wrestle with is the sovereignty of God. The simplest way to explain "sovereignty" is simply to affirm that God is in control. Period. Now, before you balk, and question my faith, please listen to *why* I am struggling with the idea of God's sovereignty. I am not questioning the superiority of God or that God is Alpha and Omega. I wouldn't even question the idea that God is the ultimate source of all power. My struggle is around the concept of *control*.

God gave us free will, which means that we have the capacity to make things happen with our lives. To relinquish all control to God suggests that I must lay my will aside in order to surrender to His will. I don't think that I am in this struggle alone because, when we're completely honest, many of us don't see ourselves as clay in the Potter's hand. Many of us believe that we are the potter! In fact, I believe that is the reason I was drawn to being a potter in the first place. I wanted to see what *I* could do. To consider God using me as a vessel for His power was a foreign concept earlier in my journey. At the time, I needed to feel in control. When I took that pottery class as an elementary school student, I wasn't saved. I didn't confess that Jesus Christ was Lord even though I went to church on Christmas, Mother's Day, and Easter. See, I am CME. (This is an inside joke: CME is Christian Methodist Episcopal, but can also refer to folks who only show up at church for "Christmas," "Mother's Day," and "Easter"!) Though I wasn't yet walking with the Lord, the class that I took at Tuley Park was a training ground for what God would do with me later in life as a servant and pastor. God desired to sculpt me into a tailor-made vessel for His glory!

It wasn't until I was an adult that I began to understand more of the brokenness of life, and how I actually am the clay that God redeems and uses. My awareness of my position, as clay and not potter, changed when I realized that I was never in charge. Yes, God can do what God wants, when God wants. The freedom that we do experience in His will, however, gave me a false sense of control. It wasn't until I began making mistake after mistake that I realized God knew me better than I knew myself. God is the one who formed and shaped us from the womb. So He knows what is best for us. The prophet Jeremiah described Jehovah God directing him to the potter's house in Jeremiah chapter 18 verses 1-6:

> "This is the word that came to Jeremiah from the Lord: 'Go down to the potter's house, and there I will give you my message.' So I went down to the potter's house, and I saw him working at the wheel. But the pot he was shaping from the clay was marred in his hands; so the potter formed it into another pot, shaping it as seemed best to him. Then the word of the Lord came to me. He said, 'Can I not do with you, Israel, as this potter does?' declares the Lord. 'Like clay in the hand of the potter, so are you in my hand, Israel.'" (Jer. 18:1-6)

The writer of this biblical text offers great insight into the sovereignty of God. The Potter in this text is the Lord Almighty and the clay represents humanity. The writer reveals that the pot the Potter was shaping was from clay that had been marred. The word "marred" suggests that the clay was disfigured in the hands of God. But how is this possible if God is sovereign? If God is in control, does He not control the clay?

Though the text doesn't elaborate more on the condition of the clay, I believe that when there is a struggle for control the result is a disfigured form. Clay that was used in biblical times wasn't necessarily pure clay. It might have had rocks, twigs, and other kinds debris that could cause disfiguration. According to Jeremiah, it was the will of the potter to decide how he would handle the marred clay. R. K. Harrison explains,

> "Whenever the vessel which he was fashioning from the worked clay was disfigured by the potter's hands...frequently in the process of throwing the clay, some defect in design, size or structure would arise. The potter then squeezed the developing pot into an amorphous mass and recommenced his task of shaping the raw material into some other suitable container. Jeremiah was impressed by the control, which the potter exercised over the clay. Whatever the reasons for dissatisfaction, he took the material and worked on it until it met his specifications. In the same way, God has absolute control over His people and will dispose of their destiny according to His purposes."[5]

In His sovereignty, God often refines us into what He envisioned for our lives. When our imperfections dominate our character, our inadequacies overshadow our attributes, and our shortcomings smother our shine, God steps into our lives and refashions us until we become what He intended. For many of us, this process is painful. But if you are willing to surrender to His will, you make yourself pliable in God's hands. Yes, God sometimes

---

5   Harrison, R. K. (1973). Jeremiah and Lamentations: an introduction and commentary (Vol. 21, p. 111). Downers Grove, IL: InterVarsity Press.

breaks us so that we can be used by Him. The good news is that it doesn't matter how disfigured we may be as long as we are in the hands of God. God has a way of taking our flaws and turning them into faithfulness when we remain in His hands! God has a track record of our taking our deficiencies and transforming them into our deliverance when we remain in His hands! So when you are in a place where you can't deal with your disfigured circumstances, whisper this simple prayer, "Lord make me over again."

The potter puts one hand on the inside of the pot and one hand on the outside of the container, pressing the clay, moving his hands from top to bottom and bottom to the top. The clay is being molded and shaped in the hands of the potter. As each pot is molded uniquely in the hands of the potter, each child of God is shaped into the person God has designed. One day He is crafting coffee mugs and mixing bowls for the home. The next day, God is creating a vase for the mantle in the great room. The Potter makes each pot as He sees fit. He creates something beautiful, and something useful, when there is a need. As we are molded and refined for God's glory, we grow to accept the calling the Divine Potter has placed on our lives.

The Pinch and The Fire

Another important step in the process is the *pinch* that happens to the masterpiece. The Hebrew meaning of "pinch" is translated as "formed." The original words used in Jeremiah mean "to nip" or "pinch." This pinch happens after the Potter has formed the pot. The potter begins to separate the formed structure from the rest of lump of clay by pinching it off. This concept suggests that one is not a complete vessel until one is detached from the stuff from which one was made.

At this point in our transformation, God often separates us to bless us, so that we can be used by Him. Once we are separated out as a unique vessel, we are most ready to move into the destiny God has designed.

Once the vessel is separated from the rest of the clay, it is formed, but still not ready to be used for the purpose it was created. The vessel must be allowed to air dry to a hard state before it is placed in the fire. If moisture remains in the clay, the vessel is at risk of exploding in the kiln. The drying process would sometimes take several days, depending upon the environment and conditions. When the vessel is in this waiting phase, other vessels are being prepared to be placed in the kiln along with this container.

Perhaps you've experienced a waiting phase, or drying period. The drying period is that season between the situation that you have come out of, and the season, or situation, that God is calling you into. During this critical period, you are in between your deliverance and your promise. You are being built for a blessing. What do you do when you are in this waiting phase?

For starters, I suggest that you allow the process to strengthen you and not break you. You are in a drying period to strengthen every area that is weak and that could collapse while you are in the fire. Some areas in your life need to be stronger before you move into the next season of your life. Please don't look at your lot in life as a punishment, but see it as an opportunity to strengthen the weak places so that when your time comes, you will be more prepared to withstand the fire.

One Friday, when I watched Pam loading the kiln, there were a lot of containers that went in: pots, mugs, bowls, vases. But on Monday after school, I saw that not all of them had made it out in one piece! Many had become damaged and broken because they couldn't handle the harsh elements of the fire!

How many dreams were deferred, just because the time wasn't right?

How many projects were aborted because they'd begun in haste?

How many potential legacies were interrupted simply because they went into the fire prematurely?

Having been in ministry and leadership for more than two decades, my advice to you is to take advantage of the drying period, by developing your character while you're waiting, so that you can stand the heat of the fire. It is never the Potter's desire to see you destroyed. Rather, the Master Potter's purpose is to develop you into the person you were called to become, through fire.

The purpose of the fire is to burn away every impurity so that when you come through the fire, you will be complete. The Potter always sets the oven at the right temperature. The kiln is set hot enough to burn away everything that will not edify you and cool enough to not consume you. Remember, God's goal for your life is *formation* and not destruction. And when you come out on the other side of the fire, you can declare to all who see you that—as one who's been developed by God's grace—you have become indestructible. Even though you may become cracked or chip while you are being used, you have been made to last through the tests of time. By God's mercies we are not consumed!

As we exchange our brokenness for exceptional purpose, by trusting God with our fractured places, we are transformed into a beautiful vessel fit for God's service.

Lessons for You

As you are discovering what it means to be transformed into the person that the Master Potter designed you to be, hold on to these lessons and principles:

- Don't give up before you understand the nature of the season you're in.
- Being broken is painful but necessary.
- Trust God during the drying season and don't abort the process!
- Though as humble as muddy clay, you are still chosen to be used by the Master.

RECOGNIZE THIS

Though you may be marred from life's circumstances, you never have to stay blemished when you are in the hands of God.

DO THIS

Every day, deliberately relinquish back to God a situation that you have tried to control. Then watch for the results!

REFLECT ON THIS

- What is something that you have been struggling with that you haven't been willing to place back onto the wheel of the Potter?
- Why do you feel it's so difficult to surrender to God?
- Do you believe God is sovereign? Why or why not?
- What lessons have you learned from the story of the Potter that have convinced you to make necessary changes in your life?
- Has what you've learned in Chapter 6 helped you? If so, explain.

CHAPTER 7

Giving God the Fragments

You know my other side
I can no longer hide
Let You down so many times
Sin freshly crucifies
Thought that I had a plan
I had it all figured out
But the more that You tried
To be by my side
The more I push You out
Lord make me over
Make me over again
Time after time I failed You
Pierced your side
When they already nailed You
Jesus heal my open wounds
I just want to be more like You
Father I let You down
What's not like you just take it out
Reconcile me Jesus
I just want to please You
Wash me and make me whole
Lord make me over
Make me over again

— *Anthony C. Williams, II*

This song reminds me that *all* of us need the Lord to make us over again.

When we're shattered is when we realize that we can't put the pieces of our lives together on our own. In fact, we can quickly become so overwhelmed with all of the broken pieces that we wonder how we will even make it through the day. The fragments we live with, the rough edges, are constant reminders of our brokenness. When we find ourselves in this space, we're willing to admit that we need something more substantial to depend on than our own thoughts. We need a sense of meaning. We crave something that supersedes our ability to manage all of the pieces. This "something" we're after is the perfect power of God intervening on our behalf to make something beautiful from the fragmented piece in our lives.

Relational Leadership

The first day I arrived at Beebe Memorial Cathedral CME (BMC), a few folks asked me to promise that I wouldn't change. I assume they viewed me as someone young and energetic, full of faith, and maybe a bit idealistic. They wanted me to keep those qualities! I know they meant well, but it wasn't a promise I could make, because it would limit the possibilities God had for my life.

To commit to remaining the same limits the growth and development God has designed for us.

In the fourteen years I've served BMC, I've actually developed the understanding that I did need to change! Over the course of my tenure I've had to transition from being a *positional* leader, who's defined by the title on my business card, to being a *relational* leader, one who's defined by my relationships, if my church was going to grow and become healthy. People don't commit to titles, but they will be devoted to a relationship.

When you are a positional leader, you must constantly use the title you possess to remind those who you have been privileged to lead who you are. This style of leadership can be effective at some level, but will limit your ability to connect with those you desire to follow you for the long haul. When I arrived at BMC, I was twenty-nine years old—the average age of one my member's grandsons! As a result, I consistently had to depend on my position as pastor to establish boundaries for my leadership. It was hard to lead this way.

Later, I became a relational leader. A relational leader leads by building relationships with those who may become followers. There are certain risks involved in relational leadership, but, in my opinion, it's the most effective way to lead most people.

One risk of relational leadership is that familiarity can breed contempt. As BMC began to become a healthy church, and I transitioned to becoming a strong leader, it was paramount that I shifted into relational leadership. This change to functioning as a relational leader was paramount for my development. However, I came to it only through the hard knocks I experienced in my early years there, when we were effectively functioning as a church plant within a traditional church setting.

The church began growing that first year, as new folks joined us. But, as is often the case, along with the growth came criticism. I will testify that I had my fair share of folks in the church who were eager to criticize my leadership and my ministry. Our growth as a church exploded during my fifth and sixth year at BMC, and criticism grew right along with our numbers!

As far as my role in the community, it wasn't business as usual anymore. As I began to become known throughout the San Francisco Bay Area and beyond, there were more eyes on me. Unfortunately, nothing in my background had given me the skills or tools to navigate some of the storms of critique I weathered during that season. Navigating the rocky terrain of how people viewed me was exhausting. It felt like the larger our church became, the smaller my world became.

While growth at BMC was largely positive, our growth wasn't always embraced by other ministries that weren't seeing the same kind of growth. We were criticized by those who saw our expansion as competition, rather than viewing it as a blessing to a city in need of positive impact that had plenty of need to go around! In some ways, I was discovering that I no longer belonged solely to the members of BMC, but was rapidly becoming a community pastor. If something happened in the community—a death, an altercation with police, an emergency—I was receiving the calls. I celebrated these opportunities but also had to make adjustments to deal with the responsibility that came with assuming the mantle of leadership.

Battling Storms

The year 2016 was historic for many of the wrong reasons. But in the midst of social and political unrest, one thing I could celebrate wholeheartedly was the Chicago Cubs. I never thought I would see the Cubs win a championship in my lifetime! The Cubs had been down 1-3 in the first four games of the series, and many, including me, thought it was going to be another "wait until next year" season once again. The Cubs hadn't won a championship for 108 years, and that last game had many of us who were watching on pins and needles. They were playing game seven in Cleveland and, because we had a worship service at church that evening, I was keeping up with the score through the game notifications on my iPad. At the end of the worship experience I'd unplugged, since we were fellowshipping, and one of my members shared with a smile that the game was tied 6-6. Though I tried not to show it, I felt panicked!

I said to myself, "I know that they are not about to lose this game. They didn't wait this long to get this close and lose."

I started praying for the team because this is what I do. I pray. (Smile)

The evening at church was coming to an end and, as I started to pack my belongings to go home, I received word from one of my leaders that a storm had swept through Cleveland and the game had been delayed!

I said to myself, "Oh no, this is getting worse."

I rushed out of the church and raced home, barely staying under the speed limit. (Yes, that's my story, and I am sticking to it!) The Cubs had had to stop playing, due to the weather, but by the time I got home and turned the television on, they were playing again. They had a brand new pitcher and, much to my surprise, they won the game! I asked myself what happened when the storm came during game seven! I don't want to speculate but, based on their actions, it seemed to have been an opportunity for the team to rethink what they were facing and what was in them as an organization. The entire team had to regroup, and they were able to come back and take the game! I don't know if they would have won if the storm hadn't caused a delay in the game.

There is potential for blessing in the midst of every storm that comes into the believer's life! Or, in the words of one old adage, "Life isn't about waiting for the storm to pass, it's learning how to dance in the rain." How do you handle the storm? Dance in the rain! Storms threaten to cause fear, shake your foundation, destroy your faith, and get you off track. And although this may be Satan's purpose for your storms, God has a different purpose! He wants to calm your fears, increase your faith, strengthen your foundation, and get you on the right track! The early storms that I faced in my ministry at Beebe Memorial Cathedral gave me the chance to retool my faith so that I could continue to be faithful to the journey to which God had called me.

The Transition

During that period of transition, something was happening within our church, and something was going on within me. There was a shift happening right before our eyes. We were no longer the declining church that no one wanted to pastor or attend. We had evolved into a church that was meeting the needs of the people of God. It was no longer "us versus them," with different factions battling against one another. The church was coming together as one. Even as this shift was occurring, I was still holding my breath, waiting for the next conflict. The wounds were still fresh, and I was bracing myself for the next fight. I was certain that it was coming because this is what we did as a church. For years, it had been who we were.

However, many of those who had instigated and fought those battles within the church's walls had passed on to the other side, and many of the new faces had no reference point or context for the trauma I'd endured or the post-traumatic stress I was feeling! I was finally free to lead in the way God had called me to lead, without worry. This freedom was new for me. When I began praying to ask God if there was something that I needed to see, so that I could move beyond the space in which I was functioning, God began to speak to my heart. But He said a few things that I wasn't ready to hear.

The message I received from the Lord was clear: I was so focused on fighting, and enduring pain, that I'd forgotten about the anointing and the real reason I'd been sent to BMC. God showed met that I'd been so distracted by the pain that I almost forgot the reason I'd been called there in the first place. Pastor David Bryant, of Allen Temple CME Church, in Chicago, says, "Distraction is a killer of the anointing." If the enemy can divert you from your divine purpose, eventually he can extinguish the passion that was the reason you were called in the first place. How many times have you gotten so caught up in trying to defend your position, that you've lost sight of your purpose? How many situations have interfered with fulfilling your calling? What person or persons showed up in your life to disrupt the covenant that you made with God? How many people, who really didn't need you, blocked from you the time you needed to concentrate in His presence? A spiritual principle that has rung true in my heart has been, "When the adversary can't annihilate you, it is his job to distract you!" I was being so distracted by what had already happened that I'd taken my eyes off the possibility of what could happen.

The anointing I'd been given was to grow the church. The reason I'd been assigned to Beebe Memorial Cathedral is because Bishop Henry M. Williamson Sr. had spoken prophetically over my life. In his godly judgment, he'd said, "Son, I am sending you to the church because I believe God has called you to grow it." I couldn't have built the church if there had been no anointing from which I was to operate.

Holy Anointing

The New Testament Greek word for "anoint" is *chrio* which means "to smear or rub with oil." It also implies the consecration of someone for office or religious service. Another Greek word, *aleipho,* also means "to anoint." In the ancient near east, individuals were anointed with oil to signify God's blessing on their lives. A person was anointed for an exceptional purpose. The purpose might be to serve as a king, to lead as a prophet, to be a builder, etc. The oil was a symbol of what God was doing in the life of that person. The olive oil was made in the purest form; after the olives had been beaten, bruised, and crushed. This method was the only way to secure the oil needed for the anointing.

When I paused to notice what God had been up to, I realized that everything that we had gone through was by divine design and God had allowed it to happen to release something within us, as a church, and within me, as a leader. God's anointing didn't mean that everything was smooth sailing. But it did mean that there was divine purpose that allowed us to grow. I knew God had anointed me to be the vessel who would help to build Beebe Memorial Cathedral again. We had been through too many trials for all our work to be in vain. The tests were necessary for the anointing oil to flow in my life, and I had to be subjected to the crushing process to get there. Every struggle we endured was God allowing us to be bruised and beaten. As a result, we could be used by Him to extend the ministry beyond our brokenness.

It's Not My Own, and It Belongs to You!

In Luke's gospel, verse 12:48, Jesus announces, "From everyone who has been given much, much will be demanded; and from the one who has been entrusted with much, much more will be asked."

To a certain degree, it's good to take ownership. But it's also important to ensure that your ownership should never turn into control. When your ownership morphs into control, then you assume the role of creator and not manager. It's always a holy balancing act.

Our church was growing faster than any of us ever expected, and with that kind of explosive growth came inevitable growing pains. I didn't have the staff or budget to keep up with our growth. We had a massive amount of debt that I'd inherited, along with our conference obligations. But we were finally operating at that time above water. I was being stretched every way imaginable, and I was on the verge of burnout.

I had to have another talk with God because nothing in my seminary or pastoral experience had prepared me for what I was experiencing in ministry. Some days, I would be riding the waves of ministry like a skilled surfer and other days I would just be treading water. On the worst days I felt like I was drowning. At this point of the journey I'd say I'd finally become the Senior Pastor of Beebe Memorial Cathedral—relationally! I no longer needed to revert to positional leadership. However, there was something else that was different: I couldn't keep up with all of the demands of the ministry. In my talk with God, it was revealed to me that my leadership was on a slippery slope because I was trying to manage it all by myself.

Around the time I received my eighth annual assignment as Senior Pastor at BMC, I learned a valuable lesson: although it was *my* pastoral assignment, it was *God's* church! The burden was definitely lifted from my shoulders, and I began to carry my responsibilities in whole new way. I developed a simple prayer that I would say every time I would enter the pulpit to preach the Word of God.

Before I mounted the steps to the pulpit, I prayed, "Lord, I am not perfect, as You know. Forgive me for every one of my sins. Use me as the vessel that You created me to be for Your glory. God, I am simply Your tool to be used in Your hands. Amen." This prayer delivered me from feeling the need to be perfect in the eyes of my congregation, and also it humbly reminded me who I was in God's grand design. I am just a tool who is being used by the Father. God was blessing us beyond our wildest dreams, and the best was yet to come. But no matter how much success the church enjoyed, I would remain a tool. Not a star.

There was a significant shift happening in my life physically, emotionally and spiritually. I learned how the take the pieces of my fragmented past and tattered present and give them over to the Lord Jesus. As those who've been in abusive relationships have discovered, it's hard to let go of the very thing that hurt you, even though you know it wasn't right for you. The moment I released all of my cares and concerns back into the hands of God, He began to shape me into someone new. It felt like I'd been promoted from being a warrior, fighting an unending battle, to being a priest and prophet focused on fulfilling a holy purpose. It has been estimated that it takes five to seven years before the pastor is seen by those in the congregation as the pastor of a church. I would add that it takes six to eight years before a pastor discovers his or her *purpose* within the church. It takes this length to time not only to establish one's voice, but also to find the way in which one will impact that congregation. However, when that happens, it is a relief like no other because the pastor is no longer trying to be all things to all people. When a pastor is clear on his or her assignment, he or she can begin to walk in the authority of the God who called them to serve.

The change I experienced also happened to our family of faith at BMC. My congregation began to live as a church that was vision-led, staff- and leadership-empowered, with a focus on meeting the needs of the people. Our focus became meeting the needs of the people we served. This needs-based approach to ministry gave us the flexibility to not be limited to a particular type of ministry, but to be led by a passion to serve people. This breakthrough shifted our focus from maintenance and survival, as a Christian Methodist Episcopal church, to thriving as we embraced the calling to do God's ministry.

Mission to Thrive

When your focus as a leader is in the maintenance of the church, you have signed the death certificate for that congregation. There are only two types of churches: those that are growing and those that are dying. My focus early in my pastoral career was on scrambling to pay our connectional budget only. The impulse was motivated by a desire to not get moved by the bishop if a church wasn't able to pay those dues. Conference assessments, those dues we paid that represented each member of our church, is a vital part of the health of the connectional church, but it should never compromise the mission of the local church. Paying conference was good stewardship, but it has no correlation as to whether or not the church is living out its purpose.

Our members became excited about doing the work to serve the community as opposed to being annoyed by the conference budget being asked of them each year. Our mindset about our purpose had clearly grown. The beautiful result was that there were people walking down the aisle, wanting to be a part of our community of faith. Our fellowship became contagious all because we decided that BMC was God's church and was our assignment. That was the shift! It became our duty to follow the playbook of ministry, obeying God's coaching, and we left it to God to grow BMC the way He desired. This approach to ministry was liberating because servanthood became part of our cultural DNA. We strove to be excellent in everything we did. We decided that mediocrity would not work for the kingdom of God. When this mindset unified our church it became clear that the days of survival and fighting that had plagued us would soon be a distant memory of days past.

That shift not only happened in my heart and mind, and in the congregation's lives, but it was also reflected in my preaching. At one point in ministry I had struggled constantly to hear from God and find a word that would speak to the people on Sunday morning. I used to be concerned about what "they" weren't doing right and how I needed to help "them" get it right. When I gave the Lord back His ministry and His church, I no longer had the responsibility to play God. The focus of my preaching began to center on the needs of the people that I served, as well as everyday, relevant life issues. This shift gave me an unending catalog from which to preach, and it allowed me to connect to individuals in a way that I had never done previously. My purpose became preaching the good news of Jesus the Christ! And I don't mean just *some* of the times that I preached. I mean *all* of the time, because the people needed to hear it at every opportunity. It also became important to me that I my preaching had a social justice emphasis, because the New Testament convinced me that Jesus did!

I learned not to use this heavenly responsibility of proclaiming the good news to dwell on problems without solutions or conditions without imagination. My purpose was to speak so that father who was struggling to raise his children could remain faithful. My goal was to talk to that mother who was struggling with her self-esteem and wondering if she was still good enough. My assignment was to speak to the corporate leader who was catching hell at her office while trying to balance work and family. I had been called to preach to the person who was standing on the ledge of life ready to jump; who needed a solid reason to keep living.

It is our purpose as ministers of the gospel of Jesus Christ to give people hope and a practical way to deal with the vicissitudes of life. We have to move away from just preaching to people in order to have them shout and preach in a way that their lives are changed and behavior modified. Our focus as Christian leaders must never be centered solely on what's wrong with people. If we don't give them hope that their lives can be transformed into something better, then we haven't been faithful to our task.

When that seismic shift happened in my own heart, I could relate to my members' struggles and understand their needs. I shifted from "them versus me" to the reality of "us." I became one who needed the good news just as much as anyone else. I found myself in the middle of the preaching experience speaking directly to myself, as well as to others. This growth moment was liberating because it forced me to grow in the same manner as my community of faith.

I am grateful and privileged to serve the church called Beebe Memorial Cathedral. Before I'd arrived, it had been a church that several pastors turned down. Invited by former bishops, they'd chosen not to serve as senior pastor. One of the church's previous pastors even resigned on Palm Sunday, never making it to Easter! Over twenty years, it was a church that couldn't keep a leader for more than three years at a time. But look at what the Lord has done. God did it. I must say this again: God did it. God turned around a struggling church, with a significant amount of debt and dwindling membership, into a vibrant testimony for the kingdom.

I love Beebe Memorial Cathedral CME. It is a church that is open to vision, generous in giving, loving in action, and favored by His mercy. It is like no other church. Today it is so welcoming that I could never imagine anyone who could not be a part of BMC. Over the last two decades, we've become a multigenerational and multidimensional church whose average age shifted from seventy-one to thirty-four! I am not bragging (smile). I mention our demographic because this shift makes it a unique find in the kingdom. Ours is a testimony that old mainline churches can be resuscitated and come back to live a vibrant life again.

I shared this part of my story, and my congregation's story, with the hope of encouraging you to not give up on your church. Whatever state your church may be in, there is a still a strong possibility that God is not through with it yet. I am speaking to the very person who has given up and said it is not going to work. I am talking to you who are serving in ministry, and your assignment is arduous. I want to encourage you not to give up. If you are on the verge of burnout, please don't give up because you are too close to the blessing of perseverance. I won't lie and say ministry is not hard work, because it is. I won't leave you disillusioned by denying that serving as a leader in the church comes with a lot of sacrifices. It does. However, I am living testimony that you will gain more than you lose. That gain may never materialize as tangible benefits you can touch or see or put in the bank, but the person that you become is priceless.

Lessons for You

- Letting go and placing your ministry in God's possession reminds you who it belongs to! God and not you!
- God specializes in divine makeovers. But once He changes you, don't go back to the version that left you broken.
- Building people is more rewarding than tearing them down!

RECOGNIZE THIS

In spite of us, God uses us as tools of transformation for His kingdom and His glory!

DO THIS

Read the next chapter and watch God work in your life.

REFLECT ON THIS

- What shift has to take place in your life in order for you to see your possibilities?
- Are you still viewing the people who you served as the enemy or competition? Why or why not?
- When was the last time you heard a sermon? How did it make you feel? Was it relevant to your needs? Why or Why Not?
- Do you feel it is possible for God to change the situation you're facing today as His servant?
- Are you ready to exchange your brokenness for extraordinary purpose?

CHAPTER 8

Exchanging Your Brokenness

I have been blessed to travel a lot, speaking in various parts of the country and, as a pastor, I try to be a good steward of the resources God gives me. Sometimes I fly early in the morning to get the best price.

I was on a flight one time that was scheduled to leave so early in the morning, that I simply could not have a discussion with anyone. That flight scheduled to leave at 5:40 am began boarding at 5:10 am. This was entirely too early to start my day of travel! But these early flights are the only way I can make it from the west coast to the east coast before the day runs out.

I had just left our church revival only hours before my flight, and I hadn't gotten much sleep. This kind of situation was a recipe for a not-so-good flight experience. I was counting on getting some rest on the flight, since I was going to be traveling several hours. The thought of catching up on a few hours gave me comfort. I didn't pay attention to my seat assignment when I checked in, and the hope of getting some extra sleep on the flight came to crashing halt based on where I was located on the plane. I was traveling on a McDonnell-Douglas 80 plane, and the aisle of this aircraft can get tight real quick. That morning my seat wasn't in the best location. I tried to stay calm by reminding myself that I had just left revival hours before! I fell into my seat, that didn't have extra leg room, exhausted.

To add insult to injury, as fellow passengers were boarding the flight, I had to negotiate the bumps and pulls from their baggage hitting me in my arm and head as they moved along down the aisle.

Thankfully, I made it through this trial without busting a blood vessel. I refused to let anything that morning steal my joy. Everything seemed to be cool as the plane filled up with passengers. I began to close my eyes and drift off into oblivion, when that moment of sleep ecstasy was interrupted with a tap on my shoulder. This lady stood with a frown on her face, glowering at me as if I'd committed a crime. She stood with the confidence that she had the right to come at me the wrong way. She stood over me with discontent on her face as she stared me down.

I said to her in a gentle baritone voice, "Excuse me, can I help you?"

My row was already full, and I couldn't figure out why she was mad at me.

She quickly retorted, "Um, excuse me, you are sitting in my seat."

Gathering my composure, I didn't respond immediately. But as I looked at her with discontent, I'm sure my eyes communicated, "I shall not be moved."

I replied to her in a continued calm voice, "Ma'am, are you sure? Because I don't believe this is the case. This boarding pass that I have says this is my seat."

I waited in anxious anticipation to see how this drama was going to unfold. She sighed very loudly as she dropped her bag on the floor, causing everyone to turn towards us and look. I kept reminding myself, "Don't lose it. Be calm. You just left the church."

She pulled out her boarding pass and waved at me saying, with frustration, "You are in my seat."

I looked at her again, didn't say a word, pulled up my phone, and show her my electronic boarding pass. She stood there stunned because she saw I wasn't moving. I refused to say anything else because I'd just left the revival where I'd acted like I was saved and filled with the Holy Ghost. The flight attendant came quickly to assist, as the woman was holding up the line.

Immovable, she began to rifle through her things as she looked for her itinerary. She quickly scanned her boarding pass again, and her face started to turn red as a beet. Truly, her reaction was so awkward.

The flight attendant asked, "What is it, ma'am?"

The passenger stood there dumbfounded because she had to say, "I have the right seat, but I am on the wrong plane."

She missed all the announcements and went through the boarding process and didn't pay attention to the number of the plane that would carry her to her destination. I later found out that she had switched her flight but hadn't thrown away the old boarding card that had her heading toward the same destination. This lady came at me in the wrong way because she didn't pay attention to the travel itinerary that would get her to right place. She genuinely thought she was right, but was wrong because she was on the wrong plane. This fiasco could have been avoided if she had taken the time to check her location. Then we both could have reached our destinations with less annoyance!

This reaction often happens when someone has experienced some level of brokenness in their life. People feel that they have a right to come at someone else in the wrong manner. It's important that, as you develop through the school of hard knocks, you know your seat assignment and the vehicle in which God has called you to ride! How you respond to life's interruptions should not be determined by your emotional disposition but your spiritual composition. Yes, many people will come at you the wrong way, because they are in the wrong place in their lives, or read your situation wrong. In spite of this, you shouldn't allow this to trigger a bad reaction because you are called to exchange your brokenness—the interruptions, the disappointments, the losses, the sin, the frustration—for God's holy purpose. God is not breaking you because of your past, but He allows you to be broken because of your future! God can always use what's wrong about a situation to teach you your greatest lesson and blessing!

Built to Last

In 2013, I was invited to a private screening of a film that made a significant impression on me. The film, called *42*, written and directed by Brian Helgeland, was about the racial integration of American major league baseball by Jackie Robinson. Jackie Robinson wore the number 42 on his uniform, and, because of Robinson's courageous barrier-crossing integration, he became the center of much controversy and hatred during his day. Robinson weathered some tough times that left him, on many days, broken. He was broken by racism, hatred, and the uncertainty that "his kind" could play the game that he loved so well.

There was one scene in the film that particularly resonated with me. Jackie was talking to his wife Rachel about being put into the 1947 Brooklyn Dodgers lineup. Playing for the team was a huge moment for him, and for history, because it was going to change the face of baseball for generations to come. Rachel, concerned for her husband, spoke words that sparked a fire within Jackie Robinson.

She said, "The closer you get, the worse they'll be. Don't let them get to you."

Jackie replies, "I won't, God built me to last."

These words leapt off the screen like I was watching the movie in 3D! It was as if he was talking directly to me. The affirmation spoke to my heart because of every experience I'd endured that was terrible and unbearable. His words renewed my courage to fight through them.

Later than evening, when I reflected on the hardships I faced throughout the years, I recognized those moments that should have caused me to quit. But I realized that God built me to last. Some of the decisions I made were huge mistakes. Yet God allowed me to survive them because God built me to last. Jackie Robinson embraced exceptional purpose because God developed him not just to survive, but to thrive. Even in unpleasant conditions. You were not created just to survive. You were made to thrive even in the worst conditions because God made you to last. When Robinson faced ugly taunts and threats, he courageously lived into his purpose. In life's broken moments you also have the opportunity to discover what you are made of because that's when God steps in, equipping you to embrace your own exceptional purpose.

In this life, you will have to face circumstances that you did not choose. It doesn't matter what background you come from or what pedigree that you hold. No one is exempt from suffering. Yet God is faithful to redeem what you've endured for the purpose of forming you into the man or woman you were destined to become. You are being constructed like the sturdiest of brick walls, to withstand the pressures that life brings you, so your testimony will stand. You were built to last.

Before it ever becomes a formidable building block that can withstand weight and pressure, a brick is made with clay and shale. The materials are mixed together and placed in an oven and heated to two thousand degrees Fahrenheit. While the two substances are in the oven, a chemical process called vitrification takes place and begins to fuse together the two materials. It isn't until the substances go through the high temperatures of the fire that they become what they were destined and designed to be.

Your Purpose

I believe God allows the unique circumstances of your life to mix in such a way that you can handle the fire. You weather the fire because there is a purpose in your life. When you have a purpose, God is continually transforming you to endure the high temperatures of life. Through this process, God transforms you into the person that He desires for you to become. Though the struggles you have faced might have caused you to give up completely, you know that there is a greater purpose in your life. The purpose God has for you is bigger than your pain, your past, or your problems. You may have heard the adage, "You don't look like what you've been through." This has been true for many people I've met. As I listen to the stories of those who've conquered obstacles to embrace their exceptional purpose, I hear and see those who are resilient. I believe it is because of this divine purpose that has been assigned to them by the Lord Almighty.

Your purpose may be to show others how to survive a tragic situation that would break them.

Your purpose may be to demonstrate how to overcome abject poverty and become a successful person.

Your purpose may be to share the gospel with those who would never hear it because they won't ever go to a church to meet Jesus.

Whatever your purpose may be, there is a reason that you haven't given up yet! There is a reason you keep moving forward! There is a reason you keep going without throwing in the towel! There is something compelling inside you, and it is called *purpose!* Whatever your purpose, I am confident that the reason you've not been destroyed is that God has assigned you a unique purpose that no one else on this earth can accomplish.

In this season of your life, I believe God is preparing to pour into you some possibilities that you cannot yet imagine. God will take you completely out of your comfort zone and move you into a sphere that you have never experienced before. Grace will take on a whole new meaning in your life, and those who are connected to you will see God's unmerited favor resting upon you. It will be exciting to see the grace of God unfold in your life. With the eyes of my heart I can already see God doing this for you, but I also know that God's favor will not come without a price.

The Purpose of Your Purpose

The older I get, the more I realize that the Lord uses the pain, the pressures, the mistakes, and the messes in our lives to grow us. In fact, these—the things we'd rather avoid!—are some of the best opportunities God has to transform us into His own image. Instead of those things making you bitter, by God's grace they can make you better. At times, life will be painful and perplexing. You are saved, but you can still lose your job. You are anointed, but someone you love can still walk out on you. You have favor, but it doesn't mean that people will treat you right. And though life can be painful and perplexing, it's also purposeful.

Every battle, every affliction, every hardship, every fear, every trouble, every heartache, and every scare you've faced has made you into the person of character and integrity that you are today! I know if I had gone through life trying to dodge all of the rough patches God has equipped me to face, I would not be the person that I am today. No one grows by playing it safe. I am not perfect, but I believe that each day that I allow God to receive and redeem my brokenness, I am closer to my purpose. The problem is that, while we're facing struggles, we can allow pain to permeate and paralyze our perspective. What you've endured may have been painful, but it made you better. The obstacle you faced may have caused you to lose your hair, compromise your lifestyle, and maybe even change your address, but what you've endured has not been without meaning. The reason for all of it was for you to embrace your exceptional purpose.

Being Ready to Receive

God declaring that you have a purpose is not enough. You need to exchange your brokenness for purpose! In the wake of the cracks and chips you've endured, you must embrace the life God has for you. For this to happen, you must be willing to receive everything that comes with exchanging your brokenness for extraordinary purpose.

The life God has ordained for you is in reach, but are you ready to receive it?

Let me explain. One day I was sitting at my computer waiting to stream one of my favorite television shows that I missed due to travel. I'd gotten my snack and my drink, and I was ready to chill. I was sitting at the computer and clicked on the application to play my video. The video player screen popped up in the center of my computer, and I began watching my show. But something went wrong.

Right in the middle of a heated scene, my screen froze and a message displayed on my computer monitor.

"Please wait; we are buffering your video stream."

This video was suddenly unavailable.

Where did it go?

When a video is buffering, it means that one's network connection can't support the requested stream of information. The content can't be transcoded fast enough for the stream, so the buffering message pops up. In other words, I thought I was equipped to receive the show, but my network connection wasn't ready to handle the amount of information that was coming to my computer.

God has shown you a vision for what your life can become when you exchange your brokenness for exceptional purpose. The challenge is that you want the entire vision—like an hour-long network show—to reveal your possibilities from beginning to end. But there was a divine interruption in what you saw as your destiny because your network connection (the mentality you brought to the situation) wasn't ready to handle it. You've understood what God wants you to do, but you don't yet know how to execute the vision. And the rest of the program is not available because your equipment can't handle it yet.

Now, back to my story. I couldn't accept the reality that my video was unavailable. So I started manipulating the browser feature. My impatience got the best of me and, as a result, the video started over from the beginning but did the same thing, paused at the same point, again. I was outdone. Frustrated, I tried again to make the video work. And it happened all over again, just as it did before.

The annoying message glowed, "Please wait...."

However, the second of the portion of the message didn't appear. I watched the spinning circle on my screen, and even noticed that the timeline below the video was moving continuously, but there was nothing on the screen. Wanting to understand what was happening, I pulled out my smartphone to do some research. And I discovered that even though I couldn't see the video, the buffering was still transcoding the video on my behalf. That means that even though I couldn't see the video, it was still being prepared for me to watch.

The light bulb came on for me, and I could see God's hand moving in my predicament. In fact, it was very similar to what God does in my life when I exchange my brokenness for the purposes He has for my life. In the early part of that process of transformation, I wasn't ready to receive my entire assignment from God. So while I thought that God had forsaken me, He was actually preparing me so that, after the unwieldy buffering process, I could receive the message and purpose God had for me.

God uses your brokenness to create something new within you. Yes, you are walking around in the same body, but when His stripes have healed you, you are made new. Yes, you appear to be the same form of a person, but when God converts your soul, you have to be ready to receive that which the Lord has created within you.

To exchange your brokenness for the extraordinary purpose God has designed for your life, there must be a refreshed version of you! The old version will not work for the blessings that God has for you. If you attempt to remain the same, and keep the same behaviors, patterns, and actions, you will fall back into your old brokenness that God longs to redeem.

The first thing required, as you're growing into the person God has designed you to be, is that you change your mentality! If you are to receive everything that God has for you in the next phase of your journey, you must let go of the thinking that caused you to remain broken in the first place. Broken thinking perpetuates broken behaviors. The famed genius Albert Einstein said, "We cannot solve our problems with the same thinking we used when we created them." This version of you, the one God is growing and using, will require a different pattern of thought to create a different reality.

A few years ago, I wanted to find resources that could benefit folks in our community who were going through some painful break-ups. The break ups had already happened, but these sisters and brothers struggled to know how to live in their new reality. As I was reading one particularly helpful book, I came across a paragraph that explained why it's hard for people who have been broken to change their patterns of behavior. In *Getting Past Your Breakup*, Susan J. Elliott explains, of her own experience,

> "Reading was painful, yet amazing. I had never read any self-help books before and had no idea that any would speak to what was broken in me. After being a foster child and an adoptee, I always felt like the odd person in every crowd—something my therapist would define as 'terminal uniqueness.' For the first time in my life, I felt hope and realized that I might actually be able to fix things I had thought were permanently broken. It also never occurred to me that my husband was part of our problem. I was still operating under the assumption that everything wrong with our marriage was my fault. My therapist would later explain to me that 'water seeks its own level,' and that your partner's flaws and issues usually go hand in hand with your own. A person chooses a partner with a similar degree of 'brokenness' and does a dance of dysfunction where they both know the steps. Therefore, one person cannot be so much healthier than the other. Healthy people do not dance with unhealthy people."[6]

I believe this is true. When you are broken, it is difficult to have a healthy relationship until you are healed. That's why God longs to receive and redeem your broken places. God redeems your fractured pieces out of love for you and for His own glory. Yes, there will still be fissures, because you are an earthen vessel God uses for His uncontainable power. But don't go back to living a shattered life. There is much more to you than what you have been. The reason your life is being mended by the hands of God is to restore you. When you are made well, you won't return to the same behaviors and habits that left you unhealthy. The negative thinking that caused your depression is no longer welcome into your home. The bad

---

6   Elliott, Susan J. (2009-04-11). *Getting Past Your Breakup*. Perseus Book Group-A. Kindle Edition.

words that used to spew out from your mouth like an unruly water hose shall no longer be a part of your vocabulary. As you change your thinking, start to feast on positive biblical affirmations that will strengthen you when you feel the sting of the cracks and chips of the past. Start speaking life as you embrace your new journey and watch the result of His favor. As you do, the buffering will stop and you can begin to enjoy the rest of the show God has prepared for you.

Mending and Maintenance

Because everyone's process is very different, no two lives mirror each other. There will be some things that work for you that may not work for the next person. But what will be consistent is the grace that God has bestowed upon you to exchange your brokenness for the purpose God's designed for your life.

To thrive in this new season, you must make time and space for self-care. Perhaps you've heard the adage that says, "Come apart before you come apart." Remember, the reason we need to come apart is because we are sometimes moving so fast that we are spinning out of control.

When you are spinning out of control, and unraveling at the seams, you will convince yourself you can't take any time off because someone will need you. But the reality is that you may be too afraid to slow down. Fear usually drives the belief you can't slow down. This behavior lends itself to maintaining broken habits. Creating a Sabbath for your rest and renewal is just as important for your well-being as eating a healthy diet. We often underestimate the need for self-care, but the reason the cracks and chips in our vessels remain broken is because we neglect our emotional and spiritual well-being.

I recommend that you slow down, recalibrate, a take some time for maintenance and self-reflection to keep your new sense of meaning and purpose intact. Sometimes when we think about self-care, we think of massages, or pricey meals out on the town, or even an exotic vacation to a tropical destination. But self-care doesn't have to be costly. It can be a simple walk through a safe part of the neighborhood. It can be taking the time to go to a local gym or YMCA and hit the steam room for thirty minutes. It may be that you make an appointment to see a therapist once a quarter to talk through the challenges and concerns you're facing. Whatever self-care routine that you develop, please be consistent.

Prayer Works

As we come to the close of this journey, moving from brokenness to extraordinary purpose, I must say that the reason my life looks different today is because of my prayer life. I am unashamed to say that prayer has changed my life. When I was at some of my lowest moments, prayer was the only thing that helped me to weather my personal brokenness.

The most important key to moving from brokenness is prayer. Simply stated: prayer works. It is the seal that kept my life from shattering when things would get tough again. I believe it is the seal and the glue God gives you to hold it all together when the enemy wishes to see you destroyed and unhappy. Prayer works not only in your circumstances, but it is also working on you. Prayer also gives you the ability to empathize with others who have been broken. It is also a spiritual opportunity to deepen meaning in your life. Prayer gives you another level of accountability and support that helps you to continue to walk in the power and purpose of your new life.

Prayer changes my perspective on every situation and gives me new insight on how to continue to move into the extraordinary purpose God has given me. My prayer methods are simple and I'm happy to share them with you. I don't use a lot of flowery words to impress God, because I know He knows me. I use my everyday speech to converse with the Lord and share with Him my needs. I also believe that the major difference in my prayer life is that I don't just pray my words, but I also pray His Word over every area that has been bruised or chipped or cracked or fractured through the course of my day.

My words detail my needs, but His words assure me that my needs will be met. Therefore, I don't go into a conversation with God as if He will not deliver. Instead, I expect the Lord to provide based on his Word. Isaiah declares the promise of God,

"So is my word that goes out from my mouth:
It will not return to me empty,
but will accomplish what I desire
and achieve the purpose for which I sent it."
(Isa. 55:11)

Since we are in a relationship, and I am God's child, I expect my Father to provide for my needs. I expect God to deliver on the covenantal relationship that we have. And I can report that it has been my experience that God has not once failed to meet my needs. Sometimes the results of my prayers will be the opposite of my *wishes*, but there has never been a time when God was inconsistent.

It is my wish that, as you walk boldly into the new life God has blessed you to begin, you lean on the power of prayer. It is through the precious power of prayer that God can fix that which has been broken in your life and can undo what you thought was permanently done. Now, go exchange your brokenness for the extraordinary purpose for which God has designed you.

Lessons

- When you know better, you ought to do better.
- Honor your healing process with patience and understanding.
- Change your thoughts and change your condition!
- Prayer is essential in moving you from brokenness to purpose.

RECOGNIZE THIS

God will remain a consistent force in your life. It is up to you to stay consistent with Him!

DO THIS

If this book has blessed you, please share this message and give a copy to someone who might need to realize their purpose.

REFLECT ON THIS

- What frustrates you the most about not knowing how things will unfold in your life?
- How can you live consistently beyond your moments of brokenness to experience abundant life?
- Is an abundant life possible? Why or why not?
- What does a life of extraordinary purpose look like to you?
- What do you expect from God?

Epilogue

For Leaders: Embracing Health and Purpose for Broken Churches

Peter Drucker, the late leadership guru, once said that the four hardest jobs in the United States of America are the President of the United States, a university president, a CEO of a hospital, and a pastor. He added that it was not necessarily in that order! There are a number of issues that can make these leaders' jobs difficult, but the unifying challenge is that each one of these leaders is expected to lead people beyond their current reality to a greater future. The first three positions can often carry out this expectation with an arsenal of resources at their disposal, but this is not always the case for the pastor. Many pastors struggle with a lack of resources. Many are bi-vocational, serving a church and working another job to make ends meet.

I write this epilogue as a resource to church leaders who might be struggling with brokenness, to encourage you that you can trade it for exceptional purpose. I have a passion for people and a special love for leaders, specifically church leaders. As I shared my story, I pray that parts of it served as the motivation and the boost you needed to exchange your pain, failure, exhaustion, and discouragement for God's divine provisions.

Many church leaders have asked me one question over the years, "How did you transform a dead mainline church into a healthy, thriving church living out her exceptional purpose?"

My immediate reply has always been, "God did it!"

However, many pressed further. They wanted to know what I did, as a leader, to lead the church beyond her brokenness. As they're asking, many are wondering, "Can the same thing happen for me as a church leader?"

My short answer is, "Yes!"

But I hope I have shared some principles, systems, and practices that I learned and discovered along the way that will help you begin the trading process.

My journey is not unique. Many experience brokenness over the course of a pastoral journey. I'd say that my greatest gift was imagination and vision that convinced me that my current reality didn't have to become my future. I was broken and I inherited a congregation that was broken, but God provided me with something like a "spiritual video," both of my own future and also of what the church could become.

Seed Planted

I remember the day the seed was planted into my spirit and my mind. In October 2003, Bishop John R. Bryant, retired Senior Bishop of the African Methodist Episcopal Church, held his annual conference for his AME churches at Beebe Memorial Cathedral. I had only been in the church two months, but his conference of two thousand people had filled the sanctuary! It was a sight that overwhelmed me.

I could hear God whispering to my heart, "If you endure, you will fill this church too."

I didn't know what that meant, at that the time I heard it, but God would soon reveal the meaning. I did know that my assignment was to lead the people to a place they had never been and I had never been. It was destined to be a journey of faith to exceptional purpose.

My first goal was to lead them to exchange the cultural, spiritual and mental brokenness that had become their identity. This church had idolized an era that didn't exist anymore. That glorification of "the good old' days," by members who were mostly well into their eighties, continued through my first three years at BMC. Beebe Memorial Cathedral CME (BMC) had been through short tenures of leadership, so I knew I had to commit to being at the church long-term. And the presiding bishop also had to see this pastoral assignment as one that would be long term if things were to change. In my tenure at BMC, I have served three bishops who all saw the need. Praise God! I am grateful. You can't trade up for exceptional purpose if you aren't willing to commit to the ministry for seven to ten years. Don't let the brokenness that you are living through discourage you from the purpose God's set out for you.

BMC had seldom prayed together as a church outside of worship. One of the pivotal ingredients in the congregation's journey to heal beyond its brokenness was praying together frequently. In the first five years of our pastoral relationship, we held quarterly prayer concerts where we would be locked in the sanctuary from 6 pm until 6 am. This prayer time had a profound effect on our ministry and the favor we still experience today. In my first year at BMC we a spent a significant amount of time clarifying vision and committing to move in a new direction together. Because the church had lost its purpose, and struggled weekly to pay the bills and new mortgage, the church needed leadership that wasn't afraid to take a risk.

Facing Brokenness

One of the fundamental principles that helped us trade our brokenness for exceptional purpose was admitting that we were broken. This confession helped us to see our reality so that we could exchange it for a different one. From this confession, we saw more clearly where we stood and how we needed to grow. It helped us to define our purpose, which began to drive our passion. Over the years, we developed several purpose statements to meet the immediate needs of our growing church. From these we developed a mission statement that exhorts us to "witness the Word, worship the Lord, and walk in love." This pattern for living also serves as our discipleship process.

We encourage people to share the Word of God with those who are not connected to Christ. Together we worship God, because this is why God made us. After we worship, we go out and serve our community by walking in love. By practicing our mission statement, we became a church that was relational—where love and warm friendship were experienced in worship and beyond. We became a relevant church in which members believed their problems mattered and they could expect biblical responses to their needs.

Some practical principles we learned along the way that helped us make the trade for exceptional purpose:

- Attract people to your church with loving relationships; the ones they find there will keep them there.
- Connect to people emotionally!
- Develop an atmosphere of warmth and friendliness that pervades every aspect of the church's membership and culture.
- Reinforce emotional connection by doing all things with excellence.
- Nurture healthy relationships.
- Keep hate and resentment out.
- Build relationships with centers of influence in your community! (The Mayor, Chief of Police, and the Chamber, etc.)
- Be intentional about fellowship in worship.
- Brand and promote your ministry. This must be a priority if others will know that you are there!
- Lead in spite of personal sacrifices!
- Relinquish the need for control!
- Invest in your community without expectation of immediate return.
- Love every person that is associated with your community of faith.
- Love people beyond their brokenness!

These principles are practiced today within and beyond the walls of Beebe Memorial Cathedral CME. As a result, we are living out our exceptional purpose. We grew from eighty-one members to over three thousand decisions for Christ. Our church financial picture changed a struggling $227 thousand budget, with more than one million in debt in 2003, to a $1.26 million budget while liquidating more than half of our indebtedness. Also, as stewards of the buildings we own, we invested over one million dollars in renovations to the Cathedral and Education Buildings, along with a state of the art sound system that rivals major theaters.

We are grateful for our testimony and even for all the shattered pieces that made us who we are today. I share this story because this could be your story too. I want you to know that your leadership matters. I believe God for your divine possibilities to become a reality. There is a process, and, if you surrender to the process, God will orchestrate the divine exchange program that is tailor-made for you. I am a witness that He can take the discouraging fragments of your life—and in the lives of your congregants!—and trade them for an extraordinary purpose. God did it for us and I believe He can do the same for you. Be encouraged!

About the Author

Rev. Dr. Charley Hames, Jr. is the senior pastor of the historic Beebe Memorial Cathedral (BMC) in Oakland, CA. He is the author of *Pressing Reset: When Life Forces You to Start Over Again* and *Exchange: Trading Your Brokenness for Exceptional Purpose.*

As senior pastor of BMC since 2003, Dr. Hames leads one of the fastest growing congregations in the CME church. Under his leadership, BMC has grown from eighty-one members to more than three thousand members, making it one of the premier houses of worship in the San Francisco Bay Area.

Born and raised in hard knock neighborhoods on Chicago's South side, Dr. Hames is the second child of Charley Hames Sr. and Leona Elizabeth Steadman-Hames (both deceased).

Over the years, this dedicated servant of God has been honored with opportunities and awards some might have thought unlikely for someone of such humble beginnings. He's prayed over our country's congressional leaders on Capitol Hill and been named "Pastor of the Year" by the CME 9th Episcopal District. A true champion of his community, Dr. Hames also serves as chaplain of 100 Black Men of the Bay Area, Inc., President of the National Action Network's Oakland chapter, Chairman of the board of the Oakland African-American Chamber of Commerce, and he has been a proud Life Member of Alpha Phi Alpha, Fraternity, Inc. since 1993. No stranger to the broadcast airwaves, Dr. Hames has been heard across the Bay Area as KBLX's (102.9 FM) "Voice of Inspiration" for the past twelve years.

Known as a fervent fighter for the young men of this country, Dr. Hames was among a select group of pastors and community leaders who were invited to the White House, in 2012, to discuss the killing of Trayvon Martin with President Obama. Following that meeting, CNN tapped Dr. Hames to discuss the President's response to the tragedy.

Dr. Hames received his Bachelor of Arts degree in African-American studies from Chicago State University. In 2000 he earned a Master of Divinity degree from Garrett-Evangelical Theological Seminary in Evanston, Illinois. And, in 2004, he was blessed to receive his Doctor of Ministry degree in evangelism from the Perkins School of Theology, Southern Methodist University, Dallas, Texas.

Dr. Hames is married to Lady Michelle J. Gaskill-Hames. Lady Michelle serves as a Senior Vice President and Area Manager for the Greater Southern Alameda Area with Kaiser Permanente Healthcare. He is also the proud father of two sons and one daughter: Charles Jonathon, Elijah Immanuel, and Jael Deon.

Throughout his life, Dr. Hames has seen the fulfillment of Ephesians 3:20, "Now to Him who is able to do immeasurably more than all we ask or imagine, according to His power that is at work within us." He has served God with vision and action as a gifted preacher with twenty-six years in the gospel and twenty-one years in pastoral excellence. He stands as a testament of what God can do in the life of a true believer.

CPSIA information can be obtained
at www.ICGtesting.com
Printed in the USA
FSOW02n0615220417
33282FS